Mystery Revealed

MYSTERY REVEALED

A COLLABORATIVE STUDY ON THE BOOK OF
EPHESIANS

D. JAY MARTIN, EDITOR

MORNING JOY MEDIA
POTTSTOWN, PENNSYLVANIA

Published by Morning Joy Media.

Visit morningjoymedia.com for more information on bulk discounts and special promotions, or e-mail your questions to info@morningjoymedia.com.

Design: D. Jay Martin & Debbie Capeci
Cover Artwork: Let My Prayer Rise Up *by Barbara Februar © 2024,*
www.barbarafebruar.ca

ISBN 978-1-937107-83-3 (paperback)

Printed in the United States of America

Contents

Note from the Editor

D. Jay Martin

HE BOOK OF EPHESIANS IS a gift. No other portion of the New Testament so clearly speaks to Christ's design for the church. At the very heart of this message is a vision of church unity. The church is to be united, because it is Christ's bride, his body. We are at a moment in history where Paul's message of Christian unity is indispensable. In a world of division, I long to be a member of Jesus' unified kingdom.

This book was birthed out of several converging questions. First, *what would it look like to create an immersive experience in the book of Ephesians for the church I serve?* Second, *Ephesians is a book about church unity; what would it look like to collaborate with like-minded churches to co-create a pastoral commentary?* Third, *could this be written in a way that it becomes a resource not just for a sermon series but also for Bible studies, small groups, and Sunday school classes?*

The result of these intersecting questions is this book. Each of the six chapters of Ephesians has been divided into two main sections. This study also includes an introduction written by Timothy Doering and a brief conclusion written by me.

I worked with leaders from six churches to create this resource:

- ❖ **Introduction:** Timothy Doering (Parker Ford Church and Netzer)
- ❖ **Ephesians 1:** D. Jay Martin and David Hakes (Parker Ford Church)
- ❖ **Ephesians 2:** Ernest Daniels Jr. (Christ Community Church)

- ❖ **Ephesians 3:** Tasha Hoover (Storehouse Church)
- ❖ **Ephesians 4:** Justin Boyer and Ruth Martin (Cornerstone Christian Fellowship)
- ❖ **Ephesians 5:** Matt DeMontaigne, Jen Meter, and Chris M. Slawecki (Valley View Community Church)
- ❖ **Ephesians 6:** Ryan Stockton (Marsh Creek Brethren In Christ)

What follows is a pastoral commentary. I asked each author to allow good, sound research and rich theology to inform their writing. But I also asked them not to write for an academic audience. Rather, the intended audience of this book is you. It is written by pastors for folks who want to walk with Jesus and desire to grow in their understanding of what the apostle Paul wrote in Ephesians. When I wrote my chapter, I imagined it as a conversation at a coffee shop with someone from Parker Ford Church.

So, if you're looking for a deeper dive into specific theological points or debates, this resource may leave you wanting. But if you're looking for a tool to grow in your devotion to Christ, or a resource to use with a small group, youth group, Bible study, or Sunday school class—you're in the right place.

1

The Gospel Lens of Ephesians

Tim Doering

EPHESIANS 1:1–2
[1] Paul, an apostle of Christ Jesus by the will of God, To God's holy people in Ephesus, the faithful in Christ Jesus: [2] Grace and peace to you from God our Father and the Lord Jesus Christ.

HAVE YOU EVER LOOKED UP into the night sky through a telescope? Or studied a tiny organism through a microscope? Lenses are powerful tools that aid us in studying distant stars or nearby, but incredibly small, microorganisms.

Paul's letter to the church in Ephesus offers a remarkable lens for comprehending the implications of the gospel of Jesus Christ. It is like a camera with the dual capacity of a powerful telescope and an advanced microscope. The letter helps us zoom out to reveal God's eternal purposes across the universe—exposing cosmic battles in the spiritual realm and unveiling heavenly plans at work throughout history. And it shows us how to focus in on the intimate details of Christ's transforming power within the individual human heart.

This gospel lens reveals not only the deeply personal inner workings of Christ's salvation, but also its ripple effects: how God's grace transforms marriages, families, communities, tribes, ethnicities, nations, generations, and even the relationship between heaven and earth. No other book in Scripture so profoundly links the transformation of the individual with the transformation of the world. The fact that Ephesus is the church to which Paul chose to offer this kind of gospel lens is not surprising. As we will see, this city was a clear example of how belief systems shape economic, political, and social systems, and vice versa.

In Ephesians, Paul expands upon that reality to reveal yet another dimension. There are spiritual forces at work beyond the material world. These spiritual forces often shape the thoughts and minds of human culture. This clash in the heavenlies also takes place in a human heart. Paul understood that the problems facing humanity are at the same time universal and personal.

Any news that is ultimately good must be about a Savior, a God who can address all those concerns—from the universal (telescopic view of the universe) to the deeply personal (microscopic view of the human soul). The gospel has the power to simultaneously offer redemption to individuals and direct the future remaking of the whole cosmos. The modern Western church desperately needs this vision—a gospel that speaks to the deepest needs of individuals while redeeming the grand story of God's unfolding purposes in all of humanity.

THE CHURCH IN A FRACTURED WORLD

Our current moment makes Paul's words especially urgent. Xenophobia—the fear of the "other"—is quickly becoming a defining trait of our culture. Identity camps of politics, special interests, cultural worldviews, and even denominational divisions complicate our ability to connect as fellow humans, and tragically, even relate to one another within the church. Too often, we feel the need to "vet" someone before engaging with them.

What are we afraid of? Could it be that we fear others might influence us in ways that tarnish who we are? Does engaging with different viewpoints rattle our sense of identity? Or are we afraid others will label us by association with "those people" and question our loyalty to our own tribe?

Jesus confronted these fears by stepping outside of the normal relational camps. He didn't come as a Pharisee or Sadducee. He not only associated with outsiders, but listened to them, loved them, served them, and even defended them. The life of Jesus challenges the very notion of the camps we so often build. Sometimes the people who seemed farthest from him were the very ones with whom he most identified.

While Jesus loves all humanity, he also has a specific people in mind—pictured in Scripture as a tribe, a nation, a kingdom, and a family. The purpose of this group is not exclusivity, but rather formation through his love. Jesus desires to transform his people into a community that can combat isolation, heal wounds, restore broken relationships, and tear down lines of division. This people is drawn from every tribe, tongue, and nation. The Scriptures refer to this family by many names, but the most common is "the church." In many ways, Ephesians is about the church. Anyone "in Christ" is joined into the church. The church is a group of people called to become like Jesus.

Of course, the word *church* has taken on all sorts of meanings—many of them far from what Jesus intended. For some, even the word *church* can be a triggering term. It summons experiences utterly antithetical to Christ himself: immorality, injustice, abuse, and division under the banner of his name. These wounds feel like those of a dysfunctional family, but with the added weight of spirituality and religious words attached. But to stop there would be to miss the treasure. For all its failures, history also tells a story of goodness, justice, compassion, and healing poured out through countless communities of Christians who have faithfully followed Jesus.

This is vital to understanding the letter to the Ephesians. Paul invites the believers in this great Roman city not to base their story on the predominant cultural narratives of their time, but rather on the grand story of God. These early believers sat at the intersection of several large divides. The division—because of sin—between heaven and earth and the division of Jew and Gentile. It is at these same intersections that the cross of Jesus still stands—and where the church is called to be a prophetic witness today. Paul envisions redeemed individuals being formed into a community that, together, displays the image of God as humanity was created to do. **He sees the church as the very heart of what God is forming through the salvation of individuals, with the ultimate goal of a grand unity in Christ.**

In Ephesians chapter 3, Paul describes the privilege of being a servant of "this gospel." Although he proclaimed the same gospel as the other apostles, his audience and his way of proclaiming the good news were unique. His ministry centered on announcing that the life, death, resurrection, and ascension of Jesus—and the gift of the Spirit—had made it possible for old dividing lines to be crossed. Walls of hostility are torn down in Christ. Jesus transforms once-alienated individuals into stones fitted together into God's household. This was possible only because of Christ's power to walk individuals past their fears, insecurities, and wounds into the relational flourishing God had designed for them.

THE GOSPEL IN EPHESUS

The city of Ephesus itself provides a powerful picture of the unity that is uniquely possible in the church. As the fourth-largest

4

city in the Roman Empire, it epitomized the empire's values. Built on a hill, the wealthy and esteemed lived at the top, behind gates and walls. The poorest and least valued lived at the bottom. The slave trade was one of the most lucrative industries of this thriving metropolis. Roman society was deeply rooted in status, weaving injustice into the very fabric of life. The rich and powerful were the winners. Those without privilege were necessary for labor but considered irrelevant as individuals.

The gospel of Jesus, which Paul carried throughout the empire, stood in stark contrast. Jesus taught that in his kingdom the last are first, the poor in spirit inherit the earth, and the least are loved. He dignified the overlooked, welcomed the foreigner, and declared that love for "the least of these" was love for him. All these values are key themes in Ephesians.

The Roman dream was always to rise higher in status, like Caesar, the pinnacle of humanity, achieving divinity. The gospel dream is different. Christ descended. He lowered himself, poured out his life, and spilled his blood for those who had nothing to offer him. It was more than what he taught, more than how he lived—it was what he made possible for us as individuals and communities, even in our selfishness and greed.

Ephesus was also home to a sizable Jewish community, with at least one synagogue in the city (Acts 18:19, 19:8). Paul began his ministry there, as he often did, by reasoning with the Jews before turning to the Gentiles. This Jewish presence meant that questions of identity, belonging, and faithfulness to God were likely already present in the city's religious life. It also explains why Paul makes reconciliation between Jew and Gentile such a central theme in his letter. In a town divided by status, ethnicity, and belief, the church can embody a new humanity in Christ, where the dividing wall of hostility had been torn down (Eph. 2:14).

However, proclaiming Jesus as Lord in this ancient Greco-Roman city came with significant risk. There was a dangerous mix of religions at work underneath the social and economic systems of the city. Ephesus was a thriving port town, a multicultural city with advanced technology, and an economic powerhouse. Yet none of that was Ephesus's most extraordinary claim. Ephesus was the center of worship for most of the Greek and Roman world, with shrines and temples to many of the gods.

Most strikingly, it was home to one of the Seven Wonders of the Ancient World: The Temple of Artemis (also known as the Temple of Diana). This towering temple could be seen from a great distance at sea. It was a worship destination for pilgrims from across the empire. It was also a cultural icon and a substantial source of income, as Paul learned firsthand when his message began to disrupt the established economic system (see Acts 19).

As soon as those who financially benefited from the worship of Artemis felt their profit margins being threatened by the growing Christian movement, they were able to stir up the community with a rumor that Artemis was being disrespected. A mob erupted into a crazed and hostile chant: "Great is Artemis of the Ephesians!" Their identity was clearly being threatened. The gospel posed a legitimate threat to the worship of goddesses, the imperial cult of Rome (the worship of Caesar), and all the other pagan gods honored in Ephesus. Paul proclaimed a gospel message that people of all backgrounds should worship Jesus Christ as King and Lord. But "this gospel" pointed to an exclusive hope—not one god among many. The gospel of Jesus is strong enough to defeat spiritual strongholds, upend entire societies, and to unite Jew and Gentile.

MADE NEW, MADE ONE

This gospel is transformative. Jesus stands at the intersection of personal salvation and corporate redemption. In Christ, the mountains of pride are brought low, the valleys of insecurity are lifted up, and a level path is laid for the whole community to walk together into a new shared identity. It is the highway of holiness, on which Jesus displays himself through the relationships of those who walk on it. Even the emotionally wounded and socially marginalized can travel it in safety. In Christ, all are humbled, all are healed, all are dignified, and all are treated as beloved firstborn children—not by merit or wealth, but by grace. The unity and love possible among Jesus' followers is built on Christ alone, who reigns not at a distance, but by dwelling among us and raising us to himself.

In Christ, there is no need for fear of "the other." Instead, there is the grateful celebration that we are made new and we are made one in him. This oneness is not simply individual reconciliation with God but the reconciliation of all things in Christ—families restored, communities healed, nations united, generations reconciled, and the diverse members of Christ's body joined as one. What once were walls of hostility are now building blocks of God's dwelling place. What once divided us— ethnicity, culture, class, or status—becomes a testimony to the power of Christ's peace. This is the vision of the letter to the Ephesians: a redeemed humanity gathered up in Christ, reconciled to God and to one another, and made whole as his church, the fullness of him who fills everything in every way.

PREPARING TO READ EPHESIANS

As you begin to read through the book of Ephesians, keep an eye out for the themes that reveal the heart of Paul's message:

- ❖ **God's Plans and Vision**—May you see the breathtaking scope of the gospel, as Paul unfolds God's eternal purposes for his church and his world.
- ❖ **God's Grace**—May you receive all the incredible blessings that are freely given to those who trust Christ.
- ❖ **Unity, Oneness, Reconciliation, and Collaboration**—May you notice in every chapter how God is bringing together people and communities once divided to be one in Christ.
- ❖ **The Lifestyle of the Transformed**—May you catch a glimpse of what it looks like when personal redemption blossoms into community transformation.
- ❖ **The Spiritual World**—May your eyes be opened to what is happening behind the scenes, and may you stand firm in Christ amid the unseen realities.

As you prepare to read Ephesians and this study, I encourage you to meditate on Paul's prayer from Ephesians 1:15–23:

> For this reason, ever since I heard about your faith in the Lord Jesus and your love for all God's people, I have not stopped giving thanks for you, remembering you in my prayers. I keep asking that the God of our Lord Jesus Christ, the glorious Father, may give you the Spirit of wisdom and revelation, so that you may know him better. I pray that the eyes of your heart may be enlightened in

order that you may know the hope to which he has called you, the riches of his glorious inheritance in his holy people, and his incomparably great power for us who believe. That power is the same as the mighty strength he exerted when he raised Christ from the dead and seated him at his right hand in the heavenly realms, far above all rule and authority, power and dominion, and every name that is invoked, not only in the present age but also in the one to come. And God placed all things under his feet and appointed him to be head over everything for the church, which is his body, the fullness of him who fills everything in every way.

DISCUSSION QUESTIONS

1. What excites you about this study of Ephesians?

2. What did you learn in this introduction about the city of Ephesus?

3. What themes are you most looking forward to exploring in this study?

4. Paul describes how the gospel affects the big picture of God's purposes (telescopic) and the very personal redemption of individuals (microscopic). Which view do you connect with most right now, and why?

5. Where do you notice "identity camps" or divisions in your world—at school, at work, in your community, or even in church?

6. Paul prayed that the "eyes of our hearts" would be opened (Eph. 1:18). What do you hope God helps you see more clearly as you read Ephesians?

SPIRITUAL PRACTICES TO CONSIDER FOR EPHESIANS 1:1–2

❖ When was the last time you wrote a letter? Consider writing a handwritten note to someone in your life this week. Take time to encourage them. Think of a Bible verse that you would like to bless them with. Tell them why you love them.

❖ Set aside thirty minutes to pray for your church. Pray for as many people by name as you can. Get specific in your prayers for each person the Holy Spirit brings to mind.

2

𝕴𝖉𝖊𝖓𝖙𝖎𝖙𝖞 𝕮𝖗𝖎𝖘𝖎𝖘

D. Jay Martín

EPHESIANS 1:3–14

³ Praise be to the God and Father of our Lord Jesus Christ, who has blessed us in the heavenly realms with every spiritual blessing in Christ. ⁴ For he chose us in him before the creation of the world to be holy and blameless in his sight. In love ⁵ he predestined us for adoption to sonship through Jesus Christ, in accordance with his pleasure and will—⁶ to the praise of his glorious grace, which he has freely given us in the One he loves. ⁷ In him we have redemption through his blood, the forgiveness of sins, in accordance with the riches of God's grace ⁸ that he lavished on us. With all wisdom and understanding, ⁹ he made known to us the mystery of his will according to his good pleasure, which he purposed in Christ, ¹⁰ to be put into effect when the times reach their fulfillment—to bring unity to all things in heaven and on earth under Christ.

¹¹ In him we were also chosen, having been predestined according to the plan of him who works out everything in conformity with the purpose of his will, ¹² in order that we, who were the first to put our hope in Christ, might be for the praise of his glory. ¹³ And you also were included in Christ when you heard the message of truth, the gospel of your salvation. When you believed, you were marked in him with a seal, the promised Holy Spirit, ¹⁴ who is a deposit guaranteeing our inheritance un-

13

til the redemption of those who are God's possession—to the praise of his glory.

A RADICALLY NEW IDENTITY

W HEN I WAS SIXTEEN YEARS old, I moved across the world again. For the second time in my childhood, I said goodbye to friends, classmates, and teachers. When I was nine years old my family relocated from St. Louis, Missouri, to Cagayan De Oro in the Southern Philippines. Now, a little less than seven years later, we packed up and moved back to the States.

I am what is known as a "TCK" (third-culture kid), and I have some of the quirks common to TCKs. I've never quite fit anywhere. In the Philippines I was an American. Back in the States, I was a kid who had grown up overseas, experiencing and seeing things many Americans (especially kids) never will. Sixteen-year-olds are developmentally in a stage of life when their identity is being shaped in formative ways. Add to this time of life multiple cross-world moves, and you've got the recipe for a full-on identity crisis.

In December of 2003 I transferred from a small missionary-kid school in the Philippines to a big public school in the suburbs of St. Louis. I'll never forget the disorienting feelings of that season of life as I navigated new social dynamics, cultural references I didn't understand, and ways of communicating that often confused me.

That season of change launched me into a multi-year identity reorientation. I became desperate to find out who I really was and how I fit into the world. Thankfully, Jesus grabbed hold of my heart in new ways during this time of life. The pain and confusion I experienced became a catalyst that led me deeper into the Scriptures and further into the presence of Jesus.

You don't have to be a TCK to go through an identity crisis. I'm sure you've had your own version of struggling with your identity. Wrestling through fundamental questions of personhood is a universal experience. The questions of identity become even more significant when we step into relationship with Jesus.

Those who follow Jesus go through a complete transformation of identity. To become a disciple of Jesus is to intentionally step into a new, all-encompassing reality. Each of the letters the apostle Paul wrote contain some version of this theme: You used to be something different, but then you heard the gospel, gave your allegiance to Jesus, and now you are something radically new!

Attempting to explain the importance of this total change, the apostle Paul writes his famous line, "The old is gone, the new is here" (2 Cor. 5:17). In Christ, we become something fundamentally different; we are born again.

The early Christians that the apostle Paul wrote to in Ephesus went through an identity crisis even greater than the one I experienced in my childhood. Many of them came from pagan backgrounds, marked by brutality and idolatry. They lived within a culture with an utter disregard for what we in the modern world would consider basic human rights. In rejecting their former paganism, and in their acceptance of Christ, these early Christians went through a radical transformation of their worldviews.

As Paul writes to the church in Ephesus, he wants them to be clear on this new identity, the benefits and rights that emerge from it, and the behaviors that should result from identifying as followers of Christ. After his brief introduction, Paul launches into a soaring description of some of the main blessings that are ours in Jesus.

If you are a follower of Jesus, you have received a radically transformed identity. Go back and re-read Ephesians 1:3–14. What does this passage teach about your identity in Christ?

EVERY SPIRITUAL BLESSING IN CHRIST

During my freshman year of college, I set out to memorize Ephesians 1. I am so thankful the Lord laid that on my heart. There are few verses that have played on repeat in my mind more than Ephesians 1:3 (which I memorized at the time in the ESV), "Blessed be the God and Father of our Lord Jesus Christ, who has blessed us in Christ with every spiritual blessing in the heavenly places." Consider the implications of that statement for a moment.

In Christ we—those who have been born again, made new, transformed, saved, and redeemed by Jesus—have been given full access to *every spiritual blessing in the heavenly places.* If you are a follower of Christ, every single blessing that belongs to Jesus has been given to you. This is not dependent on your skills, your gifts, your worthiness, your reputation, your gender, your age, or your previous experience. All who follow Jesus, who have this new identity in him, have full access to all the blessings of Christ.

Perhaps you have Face ID on your phone, or maybe your personal computer unlocks with your fingerprint. When we step into relationship with Jesus, we are wrapped in the righteousness of Christ, and we look so much like him—in the eyes of the Father—that it's as if his phone unlocks at our glance or touch. We have full access to all the benefits of Christ!

The list of blessings that follows in Ephesians 1:3–14 is not exhaustive (all the books in the world couldn't contain them), but it is impressive, nonetheless. In this list, Paul highlights several of the blessings in Christ that are most foundational to our new identity. Here are some of the big ones: In Christ we are *chosen, made holy and blameless, loved, predestined, adopted, redeemed through his blood, forgiven of our sins, given his grace, shown the mystery of his will, included in Christ, and filled with the Holy Spirit.* This is an incredible list, highlighting the rights that come with our new identity in Jesus.

We are loved, chosen, adopted, forgiven, redeemed, made holy, included in his deepest plans, and filled with the Holy Spirit. Can we join in with the posture of worship and thanksgiving where Paul began? "Praise be to the God and Father of our Lord Jesus Christ, who has blessed us in the heavenly realms with every spiritual blessing in Christ." What an incredible and generous Lord we serve!

CHOSEN AND PREDESTINED

I've been on a multi-year Karl Barth kick. Exciting right?! But there's a problem. The great Swiss theologian's writings are way too dense for me to read and fully comprehend. So, I'm forced to read smarter people who can translate and explain what Barth wrote about in simpler ways. Karl Barth for dummies—that's me. One of my favorite Barth scholars to read is a theologian named Marty Folsom. Folsom is publishing a series of books titled *Karl Barth's Church Dogmatics for Everyone.* When I read Folsom's writings alongside Barth, I can begin to grasp what Barth is saying about a given topic.

One of the topics Barth had a lot to write about is the issue of predestination. To get into the theological weeds on questions of predestination versus free will, God's sovereignty versus human choice, is well beyond the scope of this modest pastoral work. However, we do come face-to-face with this conversation in Ephesians 1. Paul writes, "For he chose us in him before the creation of the world" (Eph. 1:4). And "he predestined us for adoption to sonship through Jesus Christ" (Eph. 1:5). And "In him we were also chosen, having been predestined according to the plan of him who works out everything in conformity with the purpose of his will" (Eph. 1:11).

Sometimes the arguments between those who emphasize God's sovereignty versus those who emphasis God's gift of freewill boil down to whether one believes God would predestine someone for damnation. This is unfortunate, because the conversation is much richer than that and the oversimplification misses the beauty of the paradox God invites us to live in. One of Barth's main insights into the mystery of election is that God's sovereign choice and predestination always starts with, includes, and ends with the Father's election and predestination of Christ. Folsom writes,

> Barth does not argue that God chooses some for heaven and some for hell. Instead, he engages God's eternal decision in Jesus to be for all humanity—whether or not they respond. The doctrine of election is not an eternal decree that binds God's hands, keeping him from further involvement with humankind. It is God's choice to be for and with humanity as the Lord who loves in freedom . . . Election is God's choice, from before the world was made, to love his creation in Jesus. [1]

The Father first and eternally chooses the Son as the exclusive means of salvation, adoption, redemption, propitiation, atonement, and sanctification. The Son eternally and always chooses to honor the Father by submitting everything to the Father's will and reign. Barth's key point is that God's work of choice, election, and predestination is always and eternally rooted in Christ. Election is not primarily about you and me. Election is always first about Jesus. When we step into

Christ, we have entered the election of God. God's will is that none should perish, and that all would be saved (2 Peter 3:9, John 3:16).

The word Paul uses that is translated as *choice* in Ephesians 1 is an important word to meditate on for a moment. The word here is *eklegomai* and appears throughout the New Testament in some key passages. At the Mount of Transfiguration, as Jesus stands with Moses and Elijah, the voice of the Father breaks through the heavens declaring, "This is my Son, whom *I have chosen;* listen to him" (Luke 9:35, emphasis added). The same word is used of Jesus' choice of the disciples. Luke writes, "When morning came, he called his disciples to him and *chose* twelve of them" (Luke 6:13, emphasis added).

The Father has chosen the Son. The Son has chosen us. We are to choose to receive the choice that has come to us in Christ. For example, again from Luke, Jesus says, " 'Martha, Martha,' the Lord answered, 'you are worried and upset about many things, but few things are needed—or indeed only one. *Mary has chosen* what is better, and it will not be taken away from her' " (Luke 10:41–42, emphasis added).

Human adoption is a wonderful illustration of the way choice works in relationships. Brandon and Shannon Vining from Parker Ford Church (PFC) have adopted five beautiful, wonderful, complicated, and unique children. Recently at one of our PFC staff meetings, Shannon reflected on how even though she and Brandon chose to adopt these children, each of the children had to receive this choice and then, in their own way, choose to become a Vining. Legally they became Vinings on the official day of adoption. But the process of taking on the Vining identity, the values, culture, and love of the Vinings is a choice each of the children have needed to make in their own way and in their own time.

What a picture for us to ponder! Jesus has chosen us. When we give our allegiance to him, we choose into his choosing us. We love, because he first loved us (1 John 4:19).

If the election of God is not primarily about mankind's eternal destination but is first and foremost about God's choice of his own Son, then it properly centers the story of redemption back onto Jesus and his kingdom. This means we are chosen not just for our own good, we are chosen for the glory of God. Paul writes, "In him we were also chosen . . . in order that we, who were the first to put our hope in Christ, might be for the praise of his glory" (Eph. 1:11–12). The story is not about us, it is about Jesus. He is the main character, the hero, the centerpiece. When we enter that story, we step into God's chosen, predestined plan for the entire cosmos.

Whether it's for a small thing like a team captain choosing you in gym class, or a big thing like being chosen by parents for adoption, we all long to be chosen. Would you take a few minutes and thank God for choosing you to receive a new identity and all the blessings found in Jesus?

SEALED WITH THE HOLY SPIRIT

Those who are theologically minded may at this point be asking, "What role does the Spirit play in all this talk of the Father choosing the Son?" Fear not, Trinitarian friends! Paul next draws the attention of his readers to the ministry of the Holy Spirit.

Paul writes, "When you believed, you were marked in him with a seal, the promised Holy Spirit, who is a deposit guaranteeing our inheritance until the redemption of those who are God's possession" (Eph. 1:13–14). We have been fully given all these incredible blessings in Christ—redemption, adoption, forgiveness, grace, love, etc.—but what happens when we don't feel like we have access to these blessings? In this life there is suffering, doubt, and struggle. Paul desires for us to know that a day is coming when Christ will return, and the kingdom of God will be fully established on earth (1 Cor. 15). But until that day comes, whatever difficulties we face, every follower of Jesus can rest in the guarantee of our inheritance in Christ through the indwelling ministry of the Holy Spirit.

A few years into my first pastorate, an elderly woman—I'll call her Jane—who had been walking with the Lord faithfully for many years, asked if we could speak privately after the Sunday worship service. That morning, I had taught on the Holy Spirit from Romans 8 and had said something along the lines of "If you are in Christ, you have been filled with the Spirit of God." As we stepped into a private room Jane asked me if I really thought she had been filled with the Holy Spirit. I inquired, "Jane, do you love Jesus? Have you given him your heart? Do you trust him as your Lord and Savior?" "Yes!" she replied. I could confidently assure her the Scriptures are clear that everyone "in Christ" has been filled with his Spirit. Jane burst into tears of joy with an exclamation of "Wow! God has filled me with his Holy Spirit!"

Do you know that you are filled with God's Holy Spirit? Do you know that the Holy Spirit communicates continually to your spirit and soul, testifying to the will of God and the mind of Christ (Rom. 8:26–27, 1 Cor. 2:14–16)?

The New Testament has much to say about the Holy Spirit. Here are some of the most significant ministries of the Holy Spirit in our lives: the Spirit is an advocate and counselor (John 14:26), the Spirit prays for us (Rom. 8:27), the Spirit teaches us to think like Jesus (1 Cor. 2:16), the Spirit convicts us of sin (John 16:8), and the Spirit bears fruit in our lives (Gal. 5:22–25).

The Holy Spirit also acts as a guarantee of the inheritance that is ours in Christ (Eph. 1:13–14).

If you are "in Christ" you have been sealed with the Holy Spirit. You belong to God. You were purchased and ransomed by his blood. He has adopted you into his family, he gave you a new name, and he has given you continual access to every spiritual blessing in the heavenly places. All this is part of your new identity in Jesus. Take hold of it. Live into it. Walk it out.

PASTORAL ENCOURAGEMENT

I wish every follower of Jesus would take time to memorize this amazing passage of Scripture. I know this isn't feasible for everyone. But would you at the very least consider spending time this week meditating on the amazing truths promised in this Scripture? You are more loved by God than you have ever dared to believe might be true. In Christ you have been *fully* redeemed. You have also been set apart to live a holy life filled with good works that glorify God.

If you are struggling with feelings of inadequacy, put to heart these words especially:

> He chose us in him before the creation of the world to be holy and blameless in his sight. In love he predestined us for adoption to sonship through Jesus Christ, in accordance with his pleasure and will—to the praise of his glorious grace, which he has freely given us in the One he loves. In him we have redemption through his blood, the forgiveness of sins, in accordance with the riches of God's grace that he lavished on us. (Eph. 1:4–8)

DISCUSSION QUESTIONS

1. What is the biggest "identity crisis" you've been through?

2. What is our new identity in Christ?

3. What are some of the key "blessings" we all experience in Christ?

4. If these blessings saturated every aspect of your life, what would change?

5. What other stories or passages of Scripture come to mind when thinking about the Father choosing the Son and the Son choosing us?

6. What are we chosen for?

7. What role does the Holy Spirit play in our lives?

SPIRITUAL PRACTICES TO CONSIDER FOR EPHESIANS 1:3–14

❖ **Silence and Solitude.** Nothing causes us to come face to face with our insecurities and fears quite like silence and solitude. Because of this, many people avoid true solitude (not just being physically alone but being alone and quiet with no devices to distract us). It's a scary thing to face our personal fears, insecurities, and disappointments. *Would you consider spending thirty minutes this week in silence and solitude while meditating on the list of blessings that are yours in Christ?* Let the truth of these blessings, that are yours in Christ, wash over your soul and strengthen your heart.

❖ **Forgiveness.** Who do you need to forgive? Ephesians 1:3–14 lists the amazing inheritance we have in Christ, all because he has forgiven us. *Who do you need to forgive?* Forgiveness unleashes spiritual blessings in other people's lives and in our own.

3

Christ Above Everything

David Hakes

EPHESIANS 1:15–23

¹⁵ For this reason, ever since I heard about your faith in the Lord Jesus and your love for all God's people, ¹⁶ I have not stopped giving thanks for you, remembering you in my prayers. ¹⁷ I keep asking that the God of our Lord Jesus Christ, the glorious Father, may give you the Spirit of wisdom and revelation, so that you may know him better. ¹⁸ I pray that the eyes of your heart may be enlightened in order that you may know the hope to which he has called you, the riches of his glorious inheritance in his holy people, ¹⁹ and his incomparably great power for us who believe. That power is the same as the mighty strength ²⁰ he exerted when he raised Christ from the dead and seated him at his right hand in the heavenly realms, ²¹ far above all rule and authority, power and dominion, and every name that is invoked, not only in the present age but also in the one to come. ²² And God placed all things under his feet and appointed him to be head over everything for the church, ²³ which is his body, the fullness of him who fills everything in every way.

TO KNOW OR NOT TO KNOW

SOMETIMES I DREAM THAT HE is me . . . if I could be like Mike." As a kid with a basketball in my driveway, I reenacted many of Jordan's iconic shots. I'd take a shot from fifteen feet as I'm fading away. The net would swoosh. Then I'd jump as high as I could and pump my fist in the air several times while the imaginary crowd went wild. I imagined the poor Cavs heading to the locker room once again as the Bulls advanced. Other times, though I couldn't even touch the net, I would leap up in the air like I was Air Jordan flying to the rim for a huge dunk with, of course, my tongue hanging out! I tried shooting free throws with my eyes closed, which only further damaged the neighbor's hedge bushes. After working up a good sweat, I'd sit down for a break and drink some orange Gatorade.

If you can't tell, Michael Jordan is my favorite athlete of all time. Growing up, I watched countless hours of Bulls games (thanks to living in the Midwest and having access to WGN-TV). I'd read all about Mike in the Sunday sports section, in my subscription to *Sports Illustrated for Kids,* and from basketball cards that I collected. Several years ago, I was enthralled watching *The Last Dance,* a documentary about Michael Jordan. I know so much about him, like the fact that Jordan won six NBA Championships, was the NBA's Most Valuable Player five times, averaged 33 points a game, was an NBA All-Star fourteen times, won two gold medals with the Dream Team, and ended his career with 32,292 total points and 2,514 steals. Okay, those last two stats I just Googled. But I could go on and on about Jordan because I know so much about him. However, I've never met him. We've never spoken. He doesn't even know I exist.

My childhood friend Aaron, on the other hand—oh, I knew him extremely well because we spent a lot of time together growing up. We would play nearly every sport together—tennis, basketball, baseball, golf. We first became friends while on the same Little League baseball team. We rode our bikes all over our small Iowa town. On rainy days, we'd play Commodore 64 games. He would often invite himself over and even stay for dinner—my parents never seemed to mind. He came from a broken home and just loved being with our family. Whenever the home phone rang, it was often Aaron asking if I he could come over and shoot hoops or hang. I knew Aaron well, but in a particular way that I didn't know MJ.

In the next part of Paul's letter to the church in Ephesus, Paul prays for them to know God better and better. What he has in mind isn't that they would collect facts about God so they can sweep the Bible category on *Jeopardy*. His desire was that they would know God intimately, personally, and deeply because they've spent time with God. Specifically, he wants them to know God better in three ways. First, to know the hope they have in Christ. Second, to know the riches of their inheritance in Christ. Third, to know the resurrection power that is theirs.

Let's dive into this text and allow it to encourage us to also come to know God in a deeper and more profound way.

PRAY WITH PURPOSE

"Does anyone have any prayer requests?" If you hear this common prompt, you're probably at some sort of prayer gathering, Bible study, or religious meeting. If your experience is anything like mine, one by one people begin to share, requesting prayer for various medical, financial, relational, vocational, educational, and physical needs. Some are advocating for themselves while others request prayer for those they love. The list is compiled and prayer for these often-tangible items begins. Prayer continues until all the items are prayerfully addressed. But what might be missing from these times of prayer? Paul gives us a beautiful example to follow.

Following his beautiful doxology in the first half of the chapter, where he celebrates all the spiritual blessings we have in Christ, the apostle Paul turns to prayer. Setting the stage for the prayer, he shares that he has heard about their faith in the Lord Jesus and their love for all God's people. Notice how faith and love are linked together in one expression. I think it's important to note that our faith in Jesus is best expressed by a life of love for others. Paul affirms both characteristics in the lives of the Ephesians.

Have you ever met someone who claimed to be a person of faith but treated others like garbage? I've known a few. They seem like a joyful, worshipping, fervent-praying saint at church; but on the drive home, they're a road-raging, bird-flipping monster! They say they follow Jesus and are nice to converse with in-person but behind a screen online, they slice and dice with their keystrokes, spewing hateful words especially toward those who may hold other positions or perspectives.

I know there have been times in my life when my faith hasn't always been evident in my love for others. In fact, even though I'm a pastor, there have been too many Sunday afternoons and evenings when my own family has experienced an anemic love in my responses and instead experienced my short temper, selfishness, and irritability. How closely tied is your faith and love? These Ephesians lived such that their faith in Christ and love in action reverberated all the way to Paul—he states he's indeed "heard" of their faith and love. This moves Paul to gratitude for these Ephesian believers.

Around the fourth Thursday of November we tend to express our thanks to God, others, and a certain sacrificial bird. But what if we were more thankful for our Christian brothers and sisters all throughout the year and expressed our gratitude? As Paul often does, he exclaims he has not stopped giving thanks. Really, Paul? It might be slightly overstated, but I do believe Paul practiced regular times of gratitude in prayer. Here's the challenge for us—let's build in regular times of thanksgiving and then let God and others know you're thankful for them! If you think something good toward someone, say it, text it, or write it.

Notice how Paul's encouragement continues. He doesn't stop at thankfulness. He remembers their specific needs in his prayer. Notice the purpose of his prayer. This prayer for the church in Ephesus isn't that they would be able to make budget, or that the Sunday services would go well, or that they would find more volunteers for the kids' ministry, or that the softball team would win big against Colossae! This is a prayer that they would know God better and better. We would do well to pray the same things over the people in our spheres of influence. Pray this over your kids, pray this for your spouse, pray this for your congregation, pray this for your pastor—that they would know God better and better. Pray they would experience the transformative power of his presence in their lives.

Paul prays to the "glorious Father." This phrase is used only once in the New Testament and describes God as full of magnificence and weight of honor. Paul prays that this magnificent God would give them the "Spirit of wisdom and revelation." Here Paul is praying that the Holy Spirit who indwells them would do something special and powerful by filling them in ways that lead to deepened spiritual wisdom, insight, and understanding. Knowing God isn't merely an intellectual exercise. It requires a supernatural work of the Holy Spirit to reveal Christ to us in a deeper, more personal way. The goal of this revelation is to know God better. Paul then specifies three things he wants the Ephesians to understand with their "enlightened eyes." He prays they may know the hope they have in Christ, know the riches of their inheritance, and know the power God offers.

KNOW THE HOPE THEY HAVE IN CHRIST

Verse 18 includes a beautiful statement. Paul prays they would know "the hope to which he has called you." This hope is the future certainty of our salvation. It's the confident expectation of life with Christ in the New Creation, free from sin, pain, and death. It's the promise that what we enjoy now is only a sneak peak of the glory and beauty to come. This hope is not a wishful thought; it is a solid anchor for our souls in a very turbulent world.

I think Paul understood that regardless of your specific religious background, we are all hope-based creatures. We all have our hopes set on something in the future. And whatever we've placed our hope for in the future often determines how we live our lives in the present. When Paul writes, "that you may know the hope to which he has called you," I think he is teaching that you and I have been called into the great narrative of God's salvation. Your life is not an accident. There's nothing random about who you are or what's going on in your life. He's working everything for your good and his glory. That even includes the difficult times you face—these are part of his loving plan for you.

So we set our hope on Jesus, the unshakable truth of who he is, his vision, and his mission in the world. We have been called into his narrative. Because we know that one day he's going to return and will bring justice and peace to this world, this should give us a holy discontent when we see the injustices of the world today. We don't stand back. We're not passive. We engage. This is why Paul is saying to really know him better and better, we need to know the hope to which we've been called. And we need to understand that our lives are not an accident. We have been called into Christ's grand narrative.

Have the eyes of your heart been opened to see this hope to which you've been called?

KNOW THE RICHES OF HIS INHERITANCE

Paul continues, "the riches of his glorious inheritance in his holy people" (v. 18). This speaks to the incredible treasure we, as God's children, are to him. We are his possession, his prize. I think it's important to understand the "inheritance" is not what we receive from God, but what God receives in us. We are his purchased possession, redeemed at the cost of Christ's own blood. The richness of this inheritance is not in our worthiness but in the glory of the God who redeems and possesses us as his own.

This is how God sees us. We are dearly loved sons and daughters of the King. Becoming obsessed with the opinions of others is the quickest way to forget your true worth. Our true value is found exclusively in God's perspective. If you or I allow the critique of our coworkers, the comments from online "friends," or the expectations from our parents to define who we are, then we'll never really see ourselves the way God sees us. Paul is saying, because of Christ, we are holy and blameless, we are joint heirs, and we get to participate in the heavenly riches with God!

KNOW CHRIST'S POWER

Next Paul prays they would know "his incomparably great power for us who believe" (v. 19). This is where it gets really good! Paul wants us to grasp the magnitude of the power at work in us and available to us. This power is not just for a select few; it is "for us who believe."

Where do you need God's power in your life?

There are times when I need his power to just trust him. Have you ever been tempted (like I have at points) to circumvent the process, bail out, change course, take the easier path, take the off-ramp that is way more convenient and comfortable? My prayer has been, "God, give me your power to trust that you know what you're doing and will carry me through this. I can't see how this makes sense, this is difficult, this is taking too long, but help me to trust you."

The word *incomparably* in verse 19 is significant. There is no human or earthly power that can be compared to the power of God. In the remaining verses, Paul expands this thought and demonstrates the matchless power of God through Christ.

FAR ABOVE

To help us comprehend this "incomparably great power," Paul gives us the ultimate demonstration of God's authority: the resurrection and exaltation of Jesus Christ. This is the standard by which we measure God's power. First, Paul says this power is the same power that raised Christ from the dead (v. 20). Jesus, who was beaten, bloodied, and crucified, called out in a loud voice, "Father, into your hands I commit my spirit." Then took his last breath and died. His lifeless body was wrapped and buried in a tomb. But on the third day, the power of God filled his lungs with air and Jesus came back to life. This was the ultimate victory over sin, death, and the grave. No greater demonstration of power exists than the bodily resurrection of Jesus.

Paul prays for the believers in Ephesus to know God better and better so they will realize this resurrection power is available to them as well. In Romans 8:11, Paul says, "And if the Spirit of him who raised Jesus from the dead is living in you, he who raised Christ from the dead will also give life to your mortal bodies because of his Spirit who lives in you." It's humbling and encouraging for me to consider that God has given us resurrection power through his Spirit.

Second, Paul says that God also "seated him at his right hand in the heavenly realms" (v. 20). This is the position of ultimate authority and honor. Christ is not just alive; he is reigning right now, today.

Paul then describes the cosmic supremacy of Christ. He is "far above all rule and authority, power and dominion, and every name that is invoked, not only in the present age but also in the one to come" (v. 21). This is not just a theological statement; it is a declaration of Christ's total and absolute sovereignty over every spiritual and earthly power. Nothing—no demon, no government, no sickness, no fear—is outside of Christ's authority. He has been given "all things" as his footstool, and he is the "head over everything for the church" (v. 22). I deeply appreciate the two words "far above." Friends, it's not even a contest.

The people in Ephesus were aware of spiritual forces through their practice of ancient magic. They tried to control these powers by invoking the right name. When in need, they would call on the associated pagan god to provide it. If they wanted something, they would go through the right rituals, chants, incantations, say the magic words, and invoke the name of the appropriate entity. But here Paul declares that Christ is far above "every name that is invoked."

In Acts 19, you can read about the forces as work at the time Paul visited, preached, and performed miracles in Ephesus. Sorcery was practiced but, as the people began turning to Jesus, they ended up conducting a scroll-burning ceremony. It says that these sorcery scrolls were valued at 50,000 drachmas (one drachma equals one day's wages)—this is a staggering amount of money.

Today, we may not invoke the name "Artemas," but we sometimes call out other names and rely on various things hoping to get whatever it is we need. Sometimes it's just a way to escape, numb, or distract ourselves. How many times do we invoke these names: Siri, Netflix, Captain Morgan, Visa, Tramadol, Tastykake, ZYN, Facebook, ESPN, and so on. May we be a people who first call on the name that is far above all others, the name of Jesus.

God has placed all things under Christ's feet. In the ancient world, victorious kings were depicted with a foot on the necks of their defeated enemies. Paul wants us to know that Jesus has defeated his enemies and reigns as King over all other powers.

THE CHURCH IS CHRIST'S BODY

This brings us to the final and deeply encouraging part of Paul's prayer for the Ephesians. Paul concludes by saying the church is "his body, the fullness of him who fills everything in every way" (v. 23). The church is not merely a 501(c)(3) organization; it is the physical representation of Jesus on earth. We are the body through which Christ continues to act and reveal his glory. As his body, we are filled with the same resurrection power that raised him from the dead. We are not inept, powerless people; we are the dwelling place of the fullness of God. As the church, we are not defined by our weaknesses but by the fullness of Christ who dwells in us. Our mission is to be the hands and feet of Christ, living out his love and power to a watching world.

PASTORAL ENCOURAGEMENT

You and I can know God as our closest and most beloved friend. We are invited into that level of knowledge and intimacy! I pray you will press deeper into the knowledge of Christ than you ever have before. He loves you and he is calling you to continue the journey.

DISCUSSION QUESTIONS

1. How closely in sync is your faith in Jesus and love for all God's people? Is there one that is out of balance?

2. Who is one person in your life you need to thank God for? Why?

3. How do you typically pray for others? How can you intentionally pray for others to have "the Spirit of wisdom and revelation"? What would it look like to truly know God better?

4. What is one area of your life where you feel powerless? How does the truth of God's "incomparably great power" change your perspective on that struggle?

5. If the church is "the fullness of him who fills everything in every way" (v. 23), what does that imply about your role in the world? How can your life, and the life of your church, better reflect the power and authority of Christ?

SPIRITUAL PRACTICES TO CONSIDER
FOR EPHESIANS 1:15–22

✦ **Take a walk with God.** Be aware of his presence with you as you walk. Talk to him as you would a close friend. Be still and listen. Using all your senses as you walk, praise him for everything you see, smell, touch, hear, or taste that Jesus has authority and power over—call them out and worship him. Look up at the sky and acknowledge that Jesus is far above all rule, authority, power, and dominion.

✦ **Start a gratitude journal.** Take five to ten minutes at the start of the day to express thanks to God for who he is and what he's done and is even still doing in your life. If other people come to mind, thank God for those folks.

4

Grace Through Faith

Ernest Daniels Jr.

EPHESIANS 2:1–10

¹ As for you, you were dead in your transgressions and sins, ² in which you used to live when you followed the ways of this world and of the ruler of the kingdom of the air, the spirit who is now at work in those who are disobedient. ³ All of us also lived among them at one time, gratifying the cravings of our flesh and following its desires and thoughts. Like the rest, we were by nature deserving of wrath. ⁴ But because of his great love for us, God, who is rich in mercy, ⁵ made us alive with Christ even when we were dead in transgressions—it is by grace you have been saved. ⁶ And God raised us up with Christ and seated us with him in the heavenly realms in Christ Jesus, ⁷ in order that in the coming ages he might show the incomparable riches of his grace, expressed in his kindness to us in Christ Jesus. ⁸ For it is by grace you have been saved, through faith—and this is not from yourselves, it is the gift of God— ⁹ not by works, so that no one can boast. ¹⁰ For we are God's handiwork, created in Christ Jesus to do good works, which God prepared in advance for us to do.

DEAD IN SIN, ALIVE IN CHRIST

THE APOSTLE PAUL VIVIDLY DESCRIBES our condition before coming to faith in Jesus. He does this with language that is both sobering and thought-provoking. His opening phrase is striking: "dead in transgressions and sins." At first glance, this sounds strange, because physically the people were alive. But Paul is speaking with great intentionality. He's describing a spiritual reality—we were spiritually dead, cut off from God, unable to grasp his truth.

Picture this: Someone has a heart attack, collapses, and is completely unresponsive. No voice, no touch, no command can rouse them. You can yell, "Get up!" all you want, but they won't move. Unless outside help comes—a medical professional with a defibrillator who can administer CPR—they will not be revived. Paul uses this kind of imagery to describe our spiritual state. Outwardly, we seemed alive—we worked jobs, enjoyed friends, and went about daily life. But inwardly, we were lifeless to God. Just as a heart must be revived by an outside force, our spirits needed God to intervene through Christ to bring us back to life.

Paul further elaborates our condition before the miracle of salvation. He not only says we were spiritually unresponsive, but that our entire lifestyle reflected this separation. "You once walked, following the course of this world, following the prince of the power of the air" (v. 2 ESV). In Scripture, "walking" often refers to daily conduct or habitual living. Paul explains that apart from Christ, this was our path—not an occasional stumble, but a pattern of life shaped by the world's values and the enemy's influence.

I can identify with Paul's illustration of our lives as nonbelievers. I remember seasons of my own life when I was spiritually cut off from God, living as though he didn't matter and unable to receive his truth. Paul wisely shifts from "you" to "we all," including himself in this description: "all of us also lived among them at one time, gratifying the cravings of our flesh." This is significant because it shows that sin is a universal problem. No one is exempt. It is like a doctor's waiting room where people may look different on the outside, but the very fact they're all there means one thing: they're sick and in need of a physician and a remedy. Paul doesn't point fingers at us, suggesting he is exempt from this position. He sits in the waiting room too: "We all once lived in the passions of our flesh . . . and were by nature children of wrath" (v. 3 ESV). In this way, Paul strips away any notion of his own superiority. The problem of sin is not "theirs," it's ours.

To be "children of wrath" means that by nature and by choice, we lived under God's righteous judgment. It's a harsh reality; one we'd rather not face. It reminds me of that famous line from a popular movie from the 1990s, *A Few Good Men*. During a heated scene of courtroom cross-examination, Tom Cruise's character, Lieutenant Daniel Kaffee, demands, "I want the truth!" Colonel Jessup, played by Jack Nicholson, fires back, "You can't handle the truth!" Colonel Jessup's point was that Lieutenant Kaffee, with his limited experiences, is too sheltered to stomach the harsh realities of military life.

In a similar way, Paul in Ephesians 2 delivers a truth many would rather not face: we were spiritually dead, enslaved to sin, and under God's wrath. Paul doesn't soften this truth—he tells it straight. We were guilty, enslaved, condemned, powerless. This is an uncomfortable truth. It cuts against our pride. It confronts us with a reality we'd rather ignore. But unless we face that truth about our condition, we'll never fully appreciate the beauty of the most transformative reversal in all of Scripture that follows the truth of our spiritual condition: "But God."

Martin Lloyd-Jones, who first trained and practiced as a medical doctor in London before leaving medicine to fully devote himself to ministry, went on to become one of the most influential preachers and Bible expositors of the twentieth century. He once put it this way: "The gospel may be summarized in these two words: 'But God.'" Those two words change everything. We were guilty—but God. We were enslaved—but God. We were condemned—but God. Unless we come to terms with our true condition, we'll never appreciate the depth of God's mercy.

Verse 4 declares it clearly: "But God, being rich in mercy, because of the great love with which he loved us . . . " (ESV).

I can vividly remember a time in my own life when Paul's description of being "dead in trespasses and sins" wasn't just theology—it was my reality. I was moving, working, even serving faithfully, but deep down I was spiritually unresponsive. I knew about God, but I didn't know him. My heart was beating, but my spirit was flatlined.

I'll never forget one particular night where I was sitting alone in my car, wrestling with the weight of disappointment and confusion. Everything on the outside looked fine—beautiful wife and children, music ministry thriving, somewhat satisfied with where I was heading personally—but inside, I felt numb. It was as if God was a distant echo, and I couldn't hear him anymore. That's when I realized something profound: I wasn't just tired, I was spiritually lifeless. I didn't need motivation; I needed resurrection.

And that's exactly what God did. In that quiet moment, when I had nothing left to offer, his presence met me. Not in judgment, but in mercy. I didn't hear an audible voice, but I felt his Spirit breathe on me—reviving what had long been dormant. My eyes opened. My heart softened. The Word that once felt dull suddenly came alive. It was as if God himself had applied the defibrillator of grace to my soul.

That night became my "But God" moment. I was dead, but God made me alive. I was lost, but God found me. I was striving, but God gave me peace. From that point on, I understood what Paul meant when he said, "By grace you have been saved." I couldn't earn it, explain it, or reproduce it. It was pure mercy, God doing for me what I could never do for myself.

Even now, years later, every time I read Ephesians 2, I'm reminded that my story, and every believer's story, begins with death but ends with resurrection. That's the beauty of grace. That's the power of "But God."

The Bible is full of "But God" moments: "You intended to harm me, but God intended it for good" (Gen. 50:20)—Joseph speaking to his brothers, testifies that even when people intend harm, God can redeem. "My flesh and my heart may fail, but God is the strength of my heart" (Ps. 73:26)—Asaph confesses his weakness before God and leads Israel in worship, reminding us that when we are frail, God's strength sustains us. Christ died for us, "but God raised him from the dead" (Acts 13:30)— Paul preaches to Jews and Gentiles, declaring that God's saving action in raising Jesus is the foundation of the gospel. Each "But God" moment reveals that salvation and hope are never about us trying harder or doing better; they are always about God stepping in. We didn't climb up to him—he stooped down to us.

Paul lifts our eyes to the heart of the gospel: even when we were spiritually dead, God made us alive in Christ. He raised us up and seated us with him in heavenly places (Eph. 2:6). This salvation is a gift—pure grace, received through faith. No money, no good deed, and no effort could ever earn it. It had to be this way, so no one could boast. As John Calvin put it: "We are saved by grace alone—without merit—yet not without works. But the works follow after, not before."

Paul then reminds us of our new identity. We are God's workmanship—his masterpiece. Through Christ, God intentionally designed our lives with meaning and purpose. Salvation isn't just about being rescued from sin; it's also about being transformed so we may live a life that displays God's grace through love, service, and faithfulness.

That is the gospel: we were dead, but God made us alive. We were enslaved, but God set us free. We were under wrath, but God poured out mercy. Now, as his masterpiece, we walk in the good works he prepared for us long ago. And this is not something we do in our own strength. As Peter writes, "His divine power has given us everything we need for a godly life through our knowledge of him who called us by his own glory and goodness" (2 Peter 1:3). The same God who raised us, freed us, and forgave us has also equipped us. We are not left to stumble along, trying to manufacture holiness by sheer effort. Instead, God himself supplies the power, the resources, and the grace to live the new life he has called us to. The gospel is not just about what God saved us *from;* it is also about what he has empowered us *for.*

Using the *4 Keys to Hearing God's Voice* from Dr. Mark Virkler,[1] we can invite the Lord to speak to us personally about the revelation of Paul's teaching in Ephesians 2.

"But God, being rich in mercy, because of the great love with which he loved us . . . made us alive together with Christ" (Eph. 2:4–5 ESV).

Paul reminds us that we were dead in sin, enslaved, and under wrath. But God intervened with mercy, raising us to new life in Christ. Now, as his workmanship, we are called to walk in the good works he prepared for us.

4 KEYS TO HEARING GOD'S VOICE

- **Stillness**. Quiet your heart before God. Rest in his presence and remember: you were dead, but God made you alive.
- **Vision**. Picture Jesus calling you from death to life, setting you free, and placing you in heavenly places with him.
- **Spontaneity**. Notice the gentle flow of thoughts, images, or impressions from the Spirit.
- **Journaling**. Write down what you sense God saying—truths about your identity, your purpose, or the works he has prepared for you.

PROMPT FOR REFLECTION

- "Father, speak to me about the good works you prepared for me to walk in. What do you want me to step into with faith and confidence?"
- "Holy Spirit, what area of my life do you want to bring from death to life today?"
- "Jesus, show me how you see me now as your workmanship, created for good works."

DISCUSSION QUESTIONS

1. In Ephesians 2:1–3, Paul describes believers as "dead in trespasses and sins." What does spiritual death mean in this context, and how is it different from physical death?

2. Paul says we "followed the course of this world." What does that phrase reveal about the nature of sin and spiritual influence in our lives before Christ?

3. The phrase "children of wrath" is hard to hear. How does understanding God's wrath actually deepen your appreciation for his mercy?

4. Paul says, "By grace you have been saved." What does that mean to you personally today—not just theologically, but emotionally and relationally?

5. The chapter ends by calling us God's "workmanship"—his masterpiece. What does that say about your worth and purpose in Christ? How does that truth challenge how you view yourself or others?

6. The phrase "But God" marks a turning point in Scripture—and in our stories. Where do you see a "But God" moment happening right now in your life, your family, or your church?

5

One in Christ

Ernest Daniels Jr.

EPHESIANS 2:11–22

¹¹ Therefore, remember that formerly you who are Gentiles by birth and called "uncircumcised" by those who call themselves "the circumcision" (which is done in the body by human hands)— ¹² remember that at that time you were separate from Christ, excluded from citizenship in Israel and foreigners to the covenants of the promise, without hope and without God in the world. ¹³ But now in Christ Jesus you who once were far away have been brought near by the blood of Christ.

¹⁴ For he himself is our peace, who has made the two groups one and has destroyed the barrier, the dividing wall of hostility, ¹⁵ by setting aside in his flesh the law with its commands and regulations. His purpose was to create in himself one new humanity out of the two, thus making peace, ¹⁶ and in one body to reconcile both of them to God through the cross, by which he put to death their hostility. ¹⁷ He came and preached peace to you who were far away and peace to those who were near. ¹⁸ For through him we both have access to the Father by one Spirit.

¹⁹ Consequently, you are no longer foreigners and strangers, but fellow citizens with God's people and also members of his household, ²⁰ built on the foundation of the apostles and prophets, with Christ Jesus himself as the chief cornerstone. ²¹ In him the whole building is joined together and rises to be-

come a holy temple in the Lord. [22] And in him you too are being built together to become a dwelling in which God lives by his Spirit.

ONE NEW HUMANITY IN CHRIST

AUL CONTINUES WITH A CALL to remember: "Formerly you who are Gentiles . . . were separate from Christ . . . excluded from citizenship in Israel." He is speaking to Gentile believers about their former alienation. They were outside of Israel's covenant blessings, strangers to the promises of God, and without access to his presence. This reminder is not meant to shame them but to awaken gratitude within them.

Memory can be one of our greatest teachers. When we look back, it can humble us and deepen our awareness of grace. Not long ago, I drove back to my old neighborhood where I had spent most of my childhood. I spent countless hours playing wall-ball across the street at the playground or playing basketball with my friends after church. As I sat parked in my car looking at my childhood home, my mind began to race. Before getting out of the car and engaging in conversation with an old friend, I sat there as memories flooded my mind—some joyful, some painful, some even traumatic.

Yet in the middle of it all, I was struck by one overwhelming realization: the faithfulness of God had carried me through those formative experiences to arrive at the current moment. Gratitude welled up in my heart as I remembered how far God has brought me. I thought about the roads I could have taken, the mistakes that could have defined me, and the seasons when I was far from him. And yet, his hand was steady, guiding me through it all. Thankfulness rose within me, not just for the victories but also for the valleys, because even in the darkest places, I know that God's grace was present with me. Looking back, I realized that what once felt like detours or dead ends were actually steppingstones leading me closer to his purpose for my life. The further I reflected, the clearer it became. I am where I am today not because of my strength, wisdom, or willpower, but because of his mercy, his faithfulness, and his unfailing love.

Can you say it with me? "But GOD!"

Here in Ephesians 2, Paul encourages the believers in Ephesus to remember. He admonishes them to remember that once they were separated from Christ, living without hope and without God. That word *hope* stands out. To live without hope is to live without the expectation of God's goodness. Without hope, we walk through life with no anchor for the soul and no assurance of a future. Paul intentionally paints that picture so the gospel shines brighter against the dark backdrop of our past.

But Paul doesn't leave the church at Ephesus or the rest of us in that state of despair. He pivots with a triumphant declaration: "But now in Christ Jesus you who once were far away have been brought near by the blood of Christ." The gospel always carries us from darkness into light, from distance into nearness, from isolation into belonging. This is the great reversal. Jesus changes everything. With his blood, he bridges the gap, tearing down the walls of division and reconciling us to God as one new people.

As I sat outside of that old house, I thought about belonging. At some point, we all have felt the sting of being out of place—being in a room where we felt invisible, overlooked, or unwelcome. That feeling can be crushing. But Paul reminds us that in Christ, we never have to live as outsiders again. Through him, we belong. We are members of God's household, built on the foundation of the apostles and prophets, with Christ as the cornerstone that holds it all together.

So, now when I look back at my old neighborhood, I don't just see the good or the bad memories—I see the grace of God written over my story. In Christ, I belong. My own testimony echoes the heart of Paul's words to the church at Ephesus: "But now in Christ Jesus you who once were far away have been brought near by the blood of Christ."

Written by Andrae Crouch in 1962, the gospel classic "The Blood Will Never Lose Its Power" became an anthem in the 1960s and 70s. The lyrics are timeless—they speak of the power of Jesus' blood, and the strength that it provides for us.

We often sing about the blood of Jesus, but I wonder if we ever really pause to reflect on the meaning of his sacrifice. No work, no moral effort, no human achievement could ever bring us near to God. Only Jesus' blood could do that. That realization ought to stir our hearts to worship. I can almost hear Paul saying, "Stop and let this sink in—lift your hands in gratitude, because it is only by his blood that you are near."

Paul then declares another profound truth: Jesus doesn't just give peace—he *is* peace. Through his death, he broke down the dividing wall of hostility between Jews and Gentiles, creating one new humanity in the victory of his death and resurrection. In a world where division is often weaponized—through race, class, culture, politics—the cross of Christ stands as God's redeeming answer. The cross is not a barrier but an invitation. It calls us not to separation but to reconciliation, first with God as our Father, and then to each other as siblings and joint heirs with Jesus.

This truth has real, everyday implications. Wherever hostility exists—whether in marriages, families, friendships, or entire communities—the cross calls us to pursue reconciliation, for "all this is from God, who through Christ reconciled us to himself and gave us the ministry of reconciliation" (2 Cor. 5:18

ESV). Our witness as believers should echo Christ's own minis-try, proclaiming peace to both the outsider and the insider and extending the same welcome to all people that he first extended to us.

And what is the result of this reconciliation? Paul says, "Through him we both have access in one Spirit to the Father" (v. 18 ESV). This is the beauty of our new, breathtaking reality. There are no VIP passes in the kingdom of God. No spiritual elite. Every believer—no matter their background, story, or sta-tus—can approach the Father with boldness and assurance.

Paul concludes this passage with an even greater vision of our identity. We are no longer strangers and aliens, wandering aimlessly through life without a real connection to God. We are fellow citizens of God's kingdom, members of his family, and living stones in his temple. The church, the *ekklesia,* is not just an organization or a gathering—it is God's dwelling place. It is alive, holy, and knitted together by his Spirit.

This means we were never designed to live isolated lives. Christianity is not a solo journey but a shared one. Together, by the blood of Jesus, we are being built into a home where God himself chooses to dwell. What a mystery. What a gift.

Paul's words in Ephesians 2 are more than history or the-ology—they are a living Word for us today. And the best way to let them move from information to transformation is to pause and actually listen to what God wants to say to us through them.

Using Dr. Virkler's *4 Keys to Hearing God's Voice,* we can invite the Lord to speak to us personally about the revelation of Paul's teaching in Ephesians 2:

> But now in Christ Jesus you who once were far off have been brought near by the blood of Christ. (Eph. 2:13 ESV)

Paul calls us to remember our past separation—without Christ, without hope, and without God—and our present reconciliation. Now in Christ, we have been brought near by his blood. The walls of hostility have been broken down, and we are fellow citizens and members of God's household, being built into a dwelling place for his Spirit.

4 KEYS TO HEARING GOD'S VOICE

* **Stillness**. Take a moment to quiet your heart. Sit in God's presence and remember: "But God . . . " He has rescued you, brought you near, and made you his dwelling place. Breathe slowly. Be still.
* **Vision**. Fix the eyes of your heart on Jesus. Picture him tearing down the dividing wall of hostility, welcoming you into his household, and calling you his masterpiece. What do you see?
* **Spontaneity**. Pay attention to the thoughts, images, or impressions that gently come to mind. The Spirit often speaks in that still, small voice. Don't over analyze. Simply notice.
* **Journaling**. Write down what you sense the Lord saying. Maybe he wants to remind you of a "But God" moment in your past, or perhaps he wants to give you encouragement about a current wall he is tearing down in your life. Journaling anchors those whispers so they don't get lost.

PROMPT FOR REFLECTION

- ❖ "Father, what do you want to say to me about my new identity in Christ?"
- ❖ "How do you want me to walk differently now that I know I've been raised and seated with Christ?"
- ❖ "Lord, what do you want to say to me about being your masterpiece?"
- ❖ "Father, what dividing wall do you want to tear down in my heart?"

DISCUSSION QUESTIONS

1. In verses 11–12, Paul tells the Gentile believers to remember their separation from Christ. Why do you think Paul begins with remembrance instead of immediately celebrating reconciliation?

2. Paul says the Gentiles were "without hope and without God in the world." What does it look like for a person today to live without hope?

3. Verse 14 calls Jesus "our peace." What's the difference between Jesus giving peace and Jesus being peace?

4. Paul says Jesus "broke down the dividing wall of hostility." What kinds of walls still exist today—in the church, our communities, or our own hearts?

5. In a world still divided by culture, race, politics, and pride, how can the church demonstrate the unity Christ accomplished on the cross?

6. "You are fellow citizens with the saints and members of the household of God" (v. 19 ESV). What does it mean to you to belong to God's household? How does this change the way you view other believers, especially those who are different from you?

7. How can you personally contribute to the unity, peace, and health of God's dwelling place—the church?

6

𝕸𝖞𝖘𝖙𝖊𝖗𝖞 𝕽𝖊𝖛𝖊𝖆𝖑𝖊𝖉

Tasha Hoover

EPHESIANS 3:1–13

[1] For this reason I, Paul, the prisoner of Christ Jesus for the sake of you Gentiles—

[2] Surely you have heard about the administration of God's grace that was given to me for you, [3] that is, the mystery made known to me by revelation, as I have already written briefly. [4] In reading this, then, you will be able to understand my insight into the mystery of Christ, [5] which was not made known to people in other generations as it has now been revealed by the Spirit to God's holy apostles and prophets. [6] This mystery is that through the gospel the Gentiles are heirs together with Israel, members together of one body, and sharers together in the promise in Christ Jesus.

[7] I became a servant of this gospel by the gift of God's grace given me through the working of his power. [8] Although I am less than the least of all the Lord's people, this grace was given me: to preach to the Gentiles the boundless riches of Christ, [9] and to make plain to everyone the administration of this mystery, which for ages past was kept hidden in God, who created all things. [10] His intent was that now, through the church, the manifold wisdom of God should be made known to the rulers and authorities in the heavenly realms, [11] according to his eternal purpose that he accomplished in Christ Jesus our Lord. [12] In him and through faith in him we may approach God

with freedom and confidence. [13] I ask you, therefore, not to be discouraged because of my sufferings for you, which are your glory.

WE ALL LOVE A GOOD secret. Walk through a bookstore or scroll online and you'll find titles that promise hidden wisdom: *The Secret to Losing Weight. The Secret to Avoiding Aging. The Secret to Living Your Best Life.*

There's something about a secret that draws us in. Think about when someone leans close and whispers, "I want to let you in on a secret." What happens? Your pulse quickens. Your curiosity sharpens. You can't help but lean forward, eager to know what's hidden—something important, valuable, too good to miss.

As we turn the page to chapter three of Ephesians, Paul promises us a secret revealed. He promises us a mystery uncovered.

THE FERTILE GROUND OF PRAYER

The epistle of Ephesians is unique in the writings of Paul because the first three chapters are given over almost completely to prayer. **Prayer is the fertile soil of secrets revealed.** It's the fertile ground for the discovery of the mystery and meaning of faith, and it's through prayer that we explore the mystery and receive clarity of what it means to have faith in the gospel of Jesus Christ.

It reminds me of the passage in Jeremiah: "Call to me and I will answer you and tell you great and unsearchable things you do not know" (Jer. 33:3).

Jeremiah and Paul were both imprisoned when they penned these words. These words to the prophet Jeremiah were spoken by God centuries ago when he was imprisoned for telling King Zedekiah the message God instructed him to share. These words were to encourage Jeremiah to keep calling out to God, to be in constant prayer, and to continue seeking God, especially during times of persecution.

If I am honest, when I want greater clarity on something, particularly when things are difficult, I want the quickest exit ramp. The quickest way out is usually found in the form of Google or YouTube or a quick call to a friend. But God makes it clear that he is the great mystery revealer. And it's through our communication with him that the most meaningful mysteries are revealed.

My kids have become accustomed to asking Alexa their burning questions. Everything from "What's the weather like today?" to "How do you train a cat to use the toilet?" (yes, this really was a thing in our household!) to "How many stars are there in our galaxy?"

One of the current hurdles to our generation connecting with the great mystery revealer is our instant access to information—all sorts of information. And with all that information, we are tempted to believe we can control the circumstances. We can find a way to our preferred future. But often, the information we ultimately need, the information we truly desire, can only be revealed by God.

Just recently, I found myself in full-on research mode over whether to pursue an opportunity or not. I'm talking serious stuff here: I consulted my husband like a board meeting, checked in with friends as if I were running a focus group, and yes, I Google-searched like I was preparing for a TED Talk. I even made a pros and cons list that looked more organized than my grocery list.

Then, out of nowhere, a friend gently asked, "Have you asked God about this?"

And I had to admit—I had not.

There I was, hustling through every possible resource on earth, yet somehow forgot the best source of all.

The Lord is the great mystery revealer. He wants to reveal unsearchable things that we do not know. He wants to reveal mysteries to us. He wants us to come to him through prayer and petition, asking for greater revelation. Asking for wisdom. Asking for what only he can give.

Question to consider: *Are we a people of prayer as we face the mysteries of life, trusting that our heavenly Father will reveal what we need in the perfect timing?*

If mystery unfolds from prayer, then Paul's story begins with the clear vision it gave him for his situation.

PERSPECTIVE ON CURRENT REALITIES

One of the things Paul is able to do as he prays continually (1 Thess. 5:17) is to gain new perspective. Paul models so well what it is like to reframe our current difficulties based on the eternal realities of Christ Jesus. He opens this section of the text identifying his current situation—imprisonment. Most scholars believe at this time he is under actual house arrest in Rome.

He writes: "For this reason I, Paul, a prisoner . . . "

However, he adds a qualifier: "For this reason I, Paul, a prisoner of Christ Jesus on behalf of you Gentiles" (v. 1 ESV).

This is NOT how I would describe my situation if I were Paul. I might say something like:

"Hey it's me, Tasha, unjustly put under house arrest . . ." or, "Hey guys, this is Tasha, prejudicially imprisoned by the Roman empire . . . "

But Paul says: *I am a prisoner—yes—but within the sovereignty of God, I declare my current circumstances are for the glory of God.*

In no way is Paul in an "impressive" situation at this point. Those in Ephesus may have remembered the impressive start; his bold opposition to Demetrius and Artemis, the preferred god of Ephesus (Acts 19). And perhaps they may have even been impressed Paul had made his way to Rome, the big city. But no, Paul's situation was quite different. It was unimpressive.

But this isn't something he tries to hide as if it is some shameful secret. Paul doesn't mask the difficulty. He doesn't cover up the reality of his challenging circumstances but trusts the Lord will be glorified in some way through them.

This is a hard teaching. I imagine some reading these words are in very difficult circumstances: an unsatisfying job, a challenging marriage, financial strain, loss of a loved one, a chronic illness.

As we call out to Christ, he can do the unthinkable, to change our perspective so we are no longer victims, stuck, or helpless but rather within the hand of God—guided and led by the One who placed the stars in the sky. Paul reminds us that God can use all the circumstances of our lives for the furtherance of the gospel.

You may have heard the phrase "Praise God anyway." I have mixed feelings about this phrase because it is often a euphemism for "Keep your chin up" or "Don't feel sad." When used flippantly, it can send the message that we shouldn't grieve or feel emotions of frustrations or sadness.

But when not used glibly, there is a profound reality to this statement. There is power in praise. To praise God in all circumstances works to keep our eyes focused on him, to lift us out of debilitating pain and the mire of our circumstance, enabling us to see clearly and to get a vision of how God works in and through us to transform that which may be evil or destructive into something good, creative, and redemptive. This does not mean God designs and orders the events that bring pain, chaos, confusion, and suffering to us. It does mean God is with us in all circumstances and can bring good to those who love him and who seek to respond to his call according to his purposes.

This is a high call. It is an invitation for the believer to trust in the character of God—that he will move and guide, and, even during the difficulty, he can be glorified. A hallelujah can be raised. So, Paul boldly declares that he doesn't think of himself as a prisoner of Rome, but of Christ!

Which begs the question: *Have you allowed God to reveal perspective on your current reality?*

Paul goes on to say—*I've got a secret for you.*

WHAT IS THE MYSTERY?

Imagine the Creator of the entire universe leaning close—just to whisper his most wondrous news directly to you. He's got a secret for you. Your heart races and your eyes widen as he reveals this astounding truth.

Salvation, redemption, life, future, kingdom realities all can be found in King Jesus. Christ Jesus *is* the mystery. Because Christ is the mystery, the definitive revelation of the one true God, all other pseudo-mysteries—the rituals, the pseudo-gods—can be put down.

Paul pens the words this way in Colossians:

> This mystery has been kept in the dark for a long time, but now it's out in the open. God wanted everyone, not just Jews, to know this rich and glorious secret inside and out, regardless of their background, regardless of their religious standing. The mystery in a nutshell is just

> this: Christ is in you, so therefore you can look forward
> to sharing in God's glory. It's that simple (Col. 1:26–27
> MSG).

For ages, God's prophets predicted this reality, but no one truly grasped its meaning until God unveiled it through Christ. What was hidden through history is now made plain: the living Christ has chosen to dwell within each believer, inviting all people into this astonishing reality—regardless of their background or prior knowledge of God.

There are two very profound realities I want to point out about this big, beautiful secret.

The first is **Christ is available to you.** He offers to be so intimate that his very presence will dwell within you.

Don't rush past how profound this is—Christ in you means the God of infinite greatness has chosen to dwell within you, offering a hope that transforms not only your future but your present life. It is a hope that empowers, comforts, and promises glory.

Christ in you, the hope of glory.

Paul explains that this is the heart of his preaching—*the boundless riches of Christ.* The word *boundless* means far beyond what we can know. Though it is beyond what we can fully comprehend, it is not meant to be beyond our appreciation, at least in part.

Meaning, we can spend the rest of our lives considering the riches of this great mystery but still fall short of knowing all the goodness that comes with knowing and receiving Jesus.

The second profound reality is **Christ is available for everyone.** His bold, open invitation into new life is offered to every person. In Jesus, everyone—those who've never heard and those who've heard all their lives—stand on equal ground before God, receiving the same promises, the same help, the same hope.

We may not use the language of Gentile and Jew, but we often sort people with other labels—race, ethnicity, economic status, political affiliation, gender, education, or even religious background—all subtle ways of drawing lines between "us" and "them." These divisions may seem entrenched in our world, yet the mystery revealed in Christ calls us to dismantle such boundaries, recognizing that each person is invited into the family of God with equal grace and standing.

For many, when we talk about the realities of the gospel, the primary note played is "When I die, I go to heaven because of what Jesus has done for me." Along this line of thinking, the gospel is reduced to one theory of atonement.

When the gospel is reduced to an exclusive focus on the afterlife or too strictly focused on an individual, personal decision of faith, it's not the fullness of what Jesus described as the good news and the kingdom come. And it is certainly not the mystery Paul is proclaiming. Paul is saying Jesus has come, he is the answer, and he is creating a new family! And this family is going to include people who we could never imagine occupying the same space, let alone loving one another with a Christ-like love.

HOW IS THE MYSTERY REVEALED?

> His intent was that now, *through the church*, the manifold wisdom of God should be made known to the rulers and authorities in the heavenly realms, according to his eternal purpose that he accomplished in Christ Jesus our Lord. (Eph. 3:10–11, emphasis added)

Paul assigns a lofty and cosmic role to the church. The church's very existence and conduct are revealing the great mystery—both to people and to the powers "in the heavenly realms."

The church is God's plan to make the mystery of the universal invitation of Christ known to the surrounding world and the powers and principalities.

The first way the church does this is through a visible demonstration that walls and barriers of hatred and suspicion that have long since divided humanity are no longer in the good news of Jesus.

Breaking down barriers of suspicion is not easy to do in a culture drowning in contempt, a culture that dehumanizes the other, dishonoring rather than honoring. The us/them rhetoric is sadly so commonplace, everyday language is so contemptuous, that what we are called to as believers in Jesus sounds shocking.

The text is not demanding we do not see differences but rather that we grow in our understanding and appreciation of diversity. We can only do that one relationship at a time.

Before we take on the entirety of racism or sexism or elitism, let us practice simple hospitality with curiosity within our own contexts.

Curiosity demands we leave our own world (let go of the familiar, take a risk, step out), enter someone else's world (active, humble, attentive listening), and allow ourselves to be formed by others (open to their worldviews while staying firmly true to Christ).

Who, though different from you, can you invite to a coffee or meal to get to know better? If you approach the time together with curiosity, what could you learn about (and from) their story?

A great tool I first heard from Pastor Rick Warren that has been helpful in engaging in curious, intentional conversation is found in the acronym SPEAK:

- ❖ **Story:** Tell me your story.
- ❖ **Passion:** What's your passion? What gets you up in the morning?
- ❖ **Encourage:** Based on what you hear from their story and passions—encourage them.
- ❖ **Ask:** Ask what is challenging you right now? What is causing you stress or keeping you awake at night?
- ❖ **Know:** A personal prayer: Holy Spirit, what would you have me learn from this person? Because everyone has something to teach us!

The second way the church makes the invitation known is we reveal the mystery by together proclaiming Christ.

Do you remember the story in Genesis 11?

Everyone on earth spoke the same language. People started moving together and decided to build a huge tower that would reach all the way up to the sky. For what purpose? Because they wanted to make a name for themselves and show how amazing they were.

Perhaps you recall what happens next. God scatters the people. Was this because he doesn't want the people together? No, certainly not. It's because he knows it will all go sideways when we come together for our own greatness.

The power of the church is found in a group of people, imperfect, who proclaim the perfection and love of Jesus Christ. It is through a group of people, imperfect, who continually call on, proclaim, pray in the name of the powerful Jesus.

I don't know if you noticed this, but Paul says we have *boldness and access with confidence through our faith in Christ.*

We have boldness and complete access to the One who is before all things and from whom all good things find its origin.

The church is not a social club designed primarily for entertainment, socializing, or personal connections. The church is not a clique that excludes people based on personality, appearance, or status. The church is not a networking platform to form connections that advance your situation in some way. The church is not a political action committee formed around partisan goals or social ideologies. The church is not a hobby group gathered around shared interests or activities. The church is not merely a place of tradition, ritual, or going through religious motions without genuine faith. The church is a group of widely different (imperfect!) people who call on and proclaim the great mystery, that is life and life eternal found in Jesus Christ.

PASTORAL ENCOURAGEMENT

As you reflect on Paul's words, let your heart be strengthened by the truth that God's mysterious plan is not hidden from you, but graciously revealed in Christ. Whether you feel weak or unworthy, remember the boundless riches of Jesus are for all—no matter your background or circumstance. The kingdom invitation is open wide: all who trust in Christ are fully welcomed, fully loved, and made heirs together in one family.

In seasons of uncertainty or suffering, you do not walk alone. The same Spirit that revealed the mystery to Paul now dwells in you, giving boldness, confidence, and freedom to approach God. So do not lose heart. Take courage, knowing that God is working in and through you for a glory greater than you can imagine.

DISCUSSION QUESTIONS

1. How do you experience prayer as a space for gaining insight or clarity in your own journey with Jesus?

2. Paul identifies himself as a prisoner "of Christ Jesus" despite his difficult circumstances. How can this outlook help us today reframe our own hardships or challenges? What does praising God amid pain or struggle look like practically for you?

3. How can you personally practice hospitality and curiosity to break down barriers according to the text's encouragement? Who, different from you, can you invite to a coffee or meal to get to know better? Approach the time together with curiosity. What can you learn about their story? (Consider using the acronym SPEAK.)

4. How does the church stay on mission by proclaiming Christ? How can your local church better embody this vision?

5. If someone asked you, "What is the 'mystery revealed' that Paul is talking about"—how would you answer?

SPIRITUAL PRACTICES TO CONSIDER
FOR EPHESIANS 3:1–13

❖ **Prayer.** Bring your uncertainties and unanswered questions to your Father. What mysteries of life are you trying to solve by your own strength when you need his wisdom and guidance?

❖ **Conversation.** Commit to having at least one conversation this week with someone different from yourself. Use the SPEAK acronym (a helpful guide for intentional, loving dialogue) and watch how God moves through that interaction!

7

Is Your Love Tank Full?

Tasha Hoover

EPHESIANS 3:14–21

¹⁴ For this reason I kneel before the Father, ¹⁵ from whom every family in heaven and on earth derives its name. ¹⁶ I pray that out of his glorious riches he may strengthen you with power through his Spirit in your inner being, ¹⁷ so that Christ may dwell in your hearts through faith. And I pray that you, being rooted and established in love, ¹⁸ may have power, together with all the Lord's holy people, to grasp how wide and long and high and deep is the love of Christ, ¹⁹ and to know this love that surpasses knowledge—that you may be filled to the measure of all the fullness of God.

²⁰ Now to him who is able to do immeasurably more than all we ask or imagine, according to his power that is at work within us, ²¹ to him be glory in the church and in Christ Jesus throughout all generations, for ever and ever! Amen.

I HAVE BEEN MARRIED TO MY husband, Adam, for over twenty years. I still vividly remember the very first time he said those three simple words—"I love you." It wasn't a carefully planned moment or a romantic scene straight out of a movie. Instead, it slipped out unexpectedly, almost as if the weight of his feelings burst through without warning. According to my husband, as he enjoys reminding me, my face, in response to his confession, went a shade of pink, eyes wide, stunned—a deer caught in the headlights—and I muttered a pathetic . . . *"thank you."*

I have since boldly proclaimed my love for Adam many times. Over the following twenty years those words have become a quiet rhythm in our lives, spoken daily. Sometimes they are shouted joyfully across a crowded room, sometimes mumbled tiredly after long days, other times shortened to a casual "Love ya!" They have woven their way into the fabric of our everyday existence, so familiar and frequent that their true power can sometimes fade into the background noise of routine.

But then, amid the noise and the busyness, there are moments—fragile and sacred—when the world slows, and the weight of those words settles again into their original, breathtaking meaning. In those quiet pauses, the simple "I love you" is not just a phrase but a deep, burning truth that anchors the soul.

I can almost picture the apostle Paul in this moment, folding himself in fervent, impassioned prayer before the throne of the King of Kings, begging him to reveal the immensity of his unfathomable love—to make known the mystery and the miracle of grace that sustains us all. Praying the reality of this love gets so into our bones that nothing stays the same.

This heartfelt prayer begins with the phrase, "For this reason . . . " The reason is the very mystery of the gospel we just discussed: In Christ we find life, and Christ is available to each of you—indeed, to everyone! This is a reality, not a conditional truth nor is it dependent on anything else. It is a truth—whether we accept it or not—and Paul is urging, NOW, LIVE IN THIS TRUTH. Plunge yourself deeply into this reality.

Paul devotes the next three chapters of Ephesians to practical instructions for living out the gospel's realities. But before moving forward, he wants to ensure we fully grasp the reality of God's extravagant love. He prays this reality becomes so real and embodied in us that it shapes our very being—because what is "in our bones" inevitably flows out in our behavior.

As a pastor, if I had to name one of the most difficult parts of this job, it wouldn't be sermon preparation, counseling marriages, or walking alongside people in grief and doubt—it's the continual, daily reality of living fully in the overwhelming, unfathomable love of God.

Maybe that's because we have such anemic examples of love in the world around us. Many of us have experienced this type of imperfect love firsthand in families and friendships. Love that waxes and wanes with feelings or circumstances. Love that is only earned through actions or withheld as punishment. Love tied to performance or meeting expectations. Love measured by sacrifices or favors returned. Love that lasts only as long as affection or interest remains. Love that depends on moods, convenience, or benefits.

Another significant reason may be due to our linguistic limitations. We only have one word for *love* in English, so everything gets lumped together. I really love my mom. And I also really love cilantro. Which means if I say this too often, my mom must wrestle with the fact she's in a dead heat with guacamole toppings. Not okay!

In English we have one word for *love*. In Greek—which is the language the New Testament is written in—there were four primary words for love.

EROS (ἔρως): is passionate, romantic, desire-driven love— the word where we get erotic. It's attraction, chemistry, intimacy—the butterflies in your stomach and the fire in your eyes. You might say, "I *eros* you, boo."

STORGE (στοργή): is family love—the natural affection and bond between parents and children, siblings, extended family. It's the steady, taken-for-granted, "you're stuck with me and that's a good thing" kind of love. Think grandma's hug, the way a mom looks at her child, or how siblings fight but are still loyal when it counts.

PHILIA (φιλία): is brotherly love, deep friendship, mutual affection. (A friendship so loyal, even Philly's sports fans would approve!) This is a shoulder-to-shoulder connection: "I've got your back," loyalty, trust, and shared joy. It's the bond of close friends who would drop everything to help you move or sit with you in the ER.

And then there is the fourth word for love.

AGAPE (ἀγάπη): the highest, deepest form of love—sacrificial, selfless, unconditional. It's not based on convenience but rooted in action and choice. It's the love that gives without expecting anything back. It's choosing the good of another even when it costs.

Guess which one Paul uses in this text as he prays they (and by extension, we) would grasp the width, length, height, and depth of this love extended to us by Christ? If you guessed *agape*, you guessed right. *Agape* best captures and represents the love of Jesus.

Christ's *agape* is the reality that even at your worst, his unfathomable love is still for you. This is why Paul writes elsewhere, "But God demonstrates his own love for us in this: While we were still sinners, Christ died for us" (Rom. 5:8).

He wants you to know the love Christ pours out to you is not temporal, conditional, or fickle. It is steadfast, unconditional, and unchanging. It is *agape* love.

ROOTED AND ESTABLISHED

At the core of what it means to be a Christian is not ascribing to a worldview or a religion, but rather, it is entering into a relationship with the One who is love.

Paul seems to ask: *You know what is going to allow you to live as you were designed to live and love as you were designed to love? It's being rooted and established in this love of Christ.*

Rooted is an agricultural term. When a plant is firmly rooted, it is planted in the soil from which it sucks up all the nutrients it needs to live. Paul prays, *may you be so rooted that all your motivations, dreams, desires are given life from the extravagant love of God.*

Established is an architectural term. Paul says, *whatever you are building, whatever you are trying to achieve, I pray it is built on the firm foundation of God's love. Because the only way you are going to build something worth building, is if God's love is the foundation.*

BONES AND BEHAVIOR

I mentioned earlier that what is in our bones informs our behavior. It is sometimes not until I notice my behavior that I realize I am living out of something other than God's *agape* love. I find myself comparing myself to others, trying to find a sense of validation and significance. I find myself getting a bit depressed because *what do I have to offer anyway?* I start to obsessively attempt to control life, including outcomes and how people perceive me. Or I find myself arrogant or prideful because I am obviously "crushing it," particularly compared to *that* person (just being honest!).

As has been said, the *fruit* can often lead us to the *root.* What am I rooted in? Often, I'm rooted in an empty love tank.

Adam and I have three kids, and they all share one very human, very pesky trait—they misbehave. Yes, shocking, right? Sometimes, discipline is necessary.

But other times, Adam and I have noticed something different beneath the surface. There is something else that is off. We don't always get this right, but there have been times we have said, "I don't think this is about misbehavior. I think their love tank is running empty."

Instead of acting out from defiance or naughtiness, they are responding to a deeper need—a tank that's near empty and desperate to be filled. The answer in those moments isn't punishment but pouring in love.

Maybe one of us has been working long hours, or life has been especially busy, and what they really need is focused, one-on-one attention, wrapped with kind words and plenty of hugs. The incredible truth? As their love tanks fill, everything changes—they become calmer, more joyful, secure, and at peace.

When our love tank is full, everything changes. Paul is praying our love tank "may be filled to the measure of all the fullness of God." Because when the reality of God's love seeps into our bones, it changes everything, including our behavior.

When people hurt you, when they say something critical or unkind—you don't need revenge because your love tank is full.

When people disappoint you, let you down, or break promises—but you don't become bitter because your love tank is full.

When people misunderstand you, judge or misjudge your intentions—but you don't respond with defensiveness because your love tank is full.

When life throws challenges your way—stress, chaos, or uncertainty arises—but you don't lose hope because your love tank is full.

When you face rejection or exclusion—doors close or relationships shift—but you don't withdraw or despair because your love tank is full.

When you experience failure or setbacks—plans fall apart or dreams stall—but you don't give up because your love tank is full.

When people express anger or frustration toward you—but you don't respond in kind because your love tank is full.

I can picture Paul kneeling before the Father—"Oh Father, fill their love tank with the ferocity, purity, reality of your love." In Christ, it is filled. It is filled with the *agape* love of Jesus Christ.

HOW IS OUR LOVE TANK FILLED?

Love by itself is not the only virtue extolled in this text. Paul also appeals to God's power.

> I pray that out of his glorious riches he may strengthen you with power through his Spirit in your inner being, so that Christ may dwell in your hearts through faith. (Eph. 3:16–17)

Power—such a loaded word. Too often, in everyday life, it conjures images of exploitation, manipulation, coercion, or control. We've all seen power wielded harshly—houses divided, or hearts broken under its weight.

But Paul is appealing to the reality that God's power is used for love.

I was leading a Bible study recently, and there was a new believer in our group. Her faith was like a light—bright, contagious, and beautiful to witness. But one day, she came in distracted, quiet, and weighed down. At a moment of gentle concern, the small group of women asked if she was okay.

I watched as she struggled to speak—not because finding the words about her current situation was hard, but because of her fear over what would happen once she shared. Finally, she bravely and vulnerably shared, even in the face of her fear and inner conflict. At the end she said with raw honesty, "People in my life who held power—parents, leaders, those I trusted—when I opened up to them, they didn't show me God's love. Instead, they used what I shared to shame me or push me away. And this . . . this is different. It feels new. It feels strange, but I think this is what God wants for me."

The love of God met her in a powerful way through that small group of ladies as she put down her former view of love and embraced the immensity of God's love. In that moment, I saw Paul's prayer come alive—the power of God plunging her into the width, height, length, and depth of God's love. It is the power of God that immerses us into the reality of his love for us. The power of God isn't used to shame or distance, but to engulf us in the love of God.

I remember the very first time the reality of God's love truly struck me. I was fourteen years old, and I had been invited to a youth camp by a friend from school. I hadn't grown up in the church nor heard much about this Jesus guy—but as I was watching a video of Jesus slowly stumbling toward Calvary—each step heavy with pain and purpose, the profound truth hit me like a ton of bricks: He did this. All of this. For me.

It was as if he lifted me to the summit of his love, and from that vantage point I saw stretching far into the horizon the vast lengths he would go for me. That vision of sacrificial love imprinted itself on my soul, and I have never been the same since. But plumbing the depths of God's love is not a one-time thing.

I am a recovering performance junkie—someone who's long found their sense of significance and value in how well they perform. Our culture constantly reinforces this message, and I picked up on it early. People seem to like you more when you succeed, so naturally, I pushed myself to achieve more and do well. But over different seasons of life, this pursuit left me exhausted and depleted.

Recently, I found myself caught in a mini bout of that same insatiable search for legitimacy. I could feel the wheels turning, the motor running faster and faster.

Yet, I've learned to return regularly to the quiet rhythms of withdrawing to be with my Father—the One who loves me unconditionally. In a simple, whispered prayer, I asked, "Could you reveal your love to me?" And my heavenly Father, who delights in giving gifts to his children, reminded me—in what I can only describe as a big hug from the inside. The words of Scripture came to mind: "See what great love the Father has lavished on us, that we should be called children of God! And that is what we are!" (1 John 3:1).

Is the love of God truly in your bones? Is it the source from which your life flows? Is it the unshakable foundation upon which you build? If your faith feels more like head knowledge than heart experience, don't hesitate to ask him to reveal himself more fully to you. Trust that his power is always at work, not to overwhelm, but to open your eyes to the vastness of his love.

PASTORAL ENCOURAGEMENT

Remember, God can do immeasurably more than we ask or imagine. As Paul so beautifully closes his prayer, let this be our hope and our confidence:

> Now to him who is able to do immeasurably more than all we ask or imagine, according to his power that is at work within us, to him be glory in the church and in

Christ Jesus throughout all generations, for ever and ever! Amen. (Eph. 3:20–21)

May this truth sink deep into your soul, and may your journey be one of ever-deepening awe at the limitless love and power of God at work within you. The next step awaits—step forward in faith and watch what he will do.

DISCUSSION QUESTIONS

1. What stands out to you about Paul's prayer for the Ephesians in Ephesians 3:14–21? How does it shape your understanding of God's power and love?

2. How does the love of God compare to the love seen in culture or media?

3. God's love was described as something that gets "into our bones" and changes us from the inside out. Can you share an example from your life where experiencing God's love transformed your behavior or attitude?

4. What does it mean to be "rooted and established in love" practically, both in your relationship with God and with others?

5. What are some barriers you face in allowing God's love to fill you to fullness? How might you invite God more intentionally to fill your "love tank"?

SPIRITUAL PRACTICES TO CONSIDER
FOR EPHESIANS 3:14–21

Imaginative Prayer

I find a great spiritual practice to enter the Father's love is imaginative prayer. It involves using our God-given gift of our mind that can create pictures (how wild is that?!) to enter into a biblical story to see, feel, smell, and touch the reality in a new way.

So now, I invite you to take ten quiet minutes to step into the story of the Prodigal Son. What do you feel? Perhaps the warm dirt road beneath your feet. Perhaps your aching bones from sleeping among the pigs. Perhaps your grumbling tummy as you consider the last full meal you ate. What else do you feel: shame, regret, sadness?

Now imagine turning the bend to your home. A path you have walked many times before, your eyes searching the horizon. Simultaneously a sense of hope and dread growing in your heart.

Now imagine as you spot the Father on the horizon. To your surprise he begins to run toward you. As he gets closer, you see tears streaming down his face, love and joy in his eyes, arms opened wide.

Imagine the fierce, welcoming embrace of the Father, and the rich fabric of the robe of grace being gently placed over your shoulders.

Allow yourself to rest fully in that moment of forgiveness and love.

Father, as I turn my weary steps homeward, I see you standing far off in the distance. My heart trembles—not with fear, but with something strange and new: hope. Your eyes meet mine, and in them, I see a love deeper than I ever imagined possible.

I see no anger, no judgment, only a fierce and tender love—like a light burning bright, calling me home from the darkness. It is your love that breaks through my shame and silence. I am caught, not by condemnation, but by your embracing arms.

I hear your footsteps quicken as you run to meet me, and with each step, the weight of my mistakes feels lighter. I feel your arms wrap around me, washing away my doubt, my regret, my loneliness. In your eyes, I am not the son who left, but the beloved child who has come home.

As the Father clothes the son with the finest robe, I feel your love covering me—removing every scar, regret, and failure. Help me to live with the freedom of being fully known and fully loved.

Help me, Father, to trust this love as I stand before you—naked, broken, and yet fully accepted. Teach me to live in the freedom of your grace, letting your love fill my bones and overflow into every part of my life.

Thank you for loving me fiercely, for running to me, and for never giving up on me. In your love, I find my true home. Amen.

8

One Body

Justin Ryan Boyer

EPHESIANS 4:1–16

¹ As a prisoner for the Lord, then, I urge you to live a life worthy of the calling you have received. ² Be completely humble and gentle; be patient, bearing with one another in love. ³ Make every effort to keep the unity of the Spirit through the bond of peace. ⁴ There is one body and one Spirit, just as you were called to one hope when you were called; ⁵ one Lord, one faith, one baptism; ⁶ one God and Father of all, who is over all and through all and in all.

⁷ But to each one of us, grace has been given as Christ apportioned it. ⁸ This is why it says:

"When he ascended on high,
he took many captives
and gave gifts to his people."

⁹ (What does "he ascended" mean except that he also descended to the lower, earthly regions? ¹⁰ He who descended is the very one who ascended higher than all the heavens, in order to fill the whole universe.) ¹¹ So Christ himself gave the apostles, the prophets, the evangelists, the pastors and teachers, ¹² to equip his people for works of service, so that the body of Christ may be built up ¹³ until we all reach unity in the faith and in the knowledge of the Son of God and become mature, attaining to the whole measure of the fullness of Christ.

¹⁴ Then we will no longer be infants, tossed back and forth by the waves, and blown here and there by every wind of teaching and by the cunning and craftiness of people in their deceitful scheming. ¹⁵ Instead, speaking the truth in love, we will grow to become in every respect the mature body of him who is the head, that is, Christ. ¹⁶ From him the whole body, joined and held together by every supporting ligament, grows and builds itself up in love, as each part does its work.

WHAT ARE YOU SAYING?

I REMEMBER WALKING INTO THE STADIUM and thinking, *"What the heck is going on here?!"* It was year one of a collaborative outreach program in my city. A dozen churches participated along with other nonprofits. The premise was simple—celebrate the life God had given to the people of our city and provide spiritual and tangible on-ramps for the gospel to work its way into people's lives.

The landscape was diverse. A grocery giveaway was taking place over there, and a worship team was singing right next to them. A lineup of tents for blood pressure checks, prayer, snow cones, and kids' games lined the track, with other ministries spread out across the field. Thanks to the central location of the park, many people attended. It was an excellent endeavor. Churches and ministries from around the city came together for a common good and to share God's uncommon grace.

In subsequent years, the organization was streamlined. However, that first year was one of the more chaotic events I have experienced, becoming a prophetic picture of how the church does (and doesn't) work together.

The main problem was that everyone was doing their own thing with little awareness of how it fit in with their Christian neighbor next to them. One of the prayer tents was between the worship stage and another ministry playing loud music on a wireless speaker. As I walked by, the ones praying were almost yelling at those in need of intercession, just to be heard. Additionally, there were other "clanging cymbals" from different ministries calling out for attention.

We were all earnestly proclaiming the name of Jesus in different ways, but all at the same time. The result? *Nobody heard what was being said.* As we attempted to have a chorus of worship bless God, it turned into chaotic noise as we forgot to consider one another. We were unified in desire, but not in Spirit—in mission, but not one in heart. This is a picture of the fractured modern church. Ephesians 4 reveals that the mystery of many-yet-one is not an optional part of the kingdom of the gospel we can ignore.

UNCOMFORTABLE SURPRISES

As we hit the halfway mark in the letter, Paul's focus on unity sharpens. The outworking of the blessings we have in Christ starts to take form in practical and relational ways. Although there are numerous theological tie-ins, the conjunction in verse 1—*then* (NIV) or *therefore* (ESV)—can help us examine our hearts. Are we taking seriously the gospel priority to strengthen and unify the church?

- ❖ Are we allowing the Head of the church to rule over our discomfort with other believers (vv. 1:22–23)?
- ❖ When considering the good works that Christ has prepared for us (v. 2:10), do we see the togetherness of the church as a lesser work to care about?
- ❖ Do we believe we can grow in Christ and experience a more genuine sense of his presence apart from our connection to others (vv. 2:21–22)?

- ❖ Is our faith dry when considering God's ability to do something more than we can ask or imagine in bringing the church together (vv. 3:20–21)?
- ❖ When we think about living a life worthy of the calling, do we first think about personal holiness or church relationships (v. 4:1)?

Bringing the church into reconciled relationships that reveal God's glory was not an academic exercise for Paul. His imprisonment for the gospel was related to proclaiming Christ's kingship over everything, including social order. His own apocalypse with Jesus on the road to Damascus was eye-opening. God spoke to a reluctant Ananias before healing Paul's blindness about how Paul would be God's chosen instrument, proclaim Christ to the Gentiles and to the people of Israel (Acts 9:15). So much of Paul's writings can only be properly understood in light of the Jew/Gentile divide and reconciliation.

In 2021, Francis Chan wrote *Until Unity*. Chan publicly expressed that one of the most significant problems people had with it was that he didn't *define the line*. Where is the exact point we must separate from one another? Where is the tipping point into false teaching and false brethren? While these are essential questions, at this point Paul doesn't stress orthodoxy concerns, but rather orthopathy. The on-ramp to increased unity, which many of us are reluctant to take, is littered with cognitive dissonance. It includes patience, making allowance for each other's faults, and, not *just* humility, but *complete* humility, all lowliness (v. 2 NKJV).

In Christ, the oneness believers have is an already-reality meant to be walked out. Thus, Paul uses the present active verb *to keep*, or *maintain* (ESV), in verse 3. However, this already existing reality requires work, diligence, and "every effort" on our part.

That word/phrase, *every effort,* is used in a handful of other ways, and while the exhortation is for everyone, let's single out church leaders for a moment, of which I'm one. For most of us, a great deal of energy goes into making our calling and election sure (2 Peter 1:10), both in the assurance of salvation and in ministry focus. Are we also making *every effort* to keep the unity of the Spirit? We do our best, as 2 Timothy 2:15 says, to present ourselves to God as those approved, workers who do not need to be ashamed and who correctly handle the word of truth. Are we also making *every effort* to strengthen the bond of peace in our congregations, cities, and regions?

A DIFFERENT KIND OF COMMUNITY, A DIFFERENT KIND OF KING

A tension lies at the social heart of every human. We want to be our *unique* selves, and we want to *belong* to a community. The empires of this world capitalize on our desires, twist them, and market to our fears, promoting false gospels of individualism or hive-mindedness. Christ's kingdom anchors us not to temporary, shifting, cultural values, but to the triune God. The ultimate Being, in which all of existence lives and moves and has its being, is working beyond ways that we can fully understand from our limited perspective. This matters because it provides the seedbed of the body of Christ being one, yet with many members (1 Cor. 12:14; Rom. 12:4–5). Paul addresses the divisiveness that both individualism and herd mentality can create.

The apostle starts (vv. 4–6) with the binding reality of the gospel, targeting deep-seated factions from the old life. The basis of the church's unified diversity is listed in a seven-fold fashion, pointing to completion. While much ink could be spilled on the one body, hope, faith, baptism markers, a key pattern to notice is that it is the triune God (one Spirit, one Lord, one Father) weaving, connecting, holding this unity, holding us together as one. Jesus is not a polygamist with multiple brides scattered across our cities; the Father is not a franchiser, setting up a conglomerate of orphanages in the world; the Spirit is not a religious guru, setting up competitive temples.

If we are in Christ, and filled with the Spirit, if we are part of the Father's family, we are part of something larger than the isolated person. As author Ian Harber puts it, reflecting on *deconstructing self* . . .

> The primary narrative told by the world of expressive individualism is "I am my own and I belong to myself." This narrative of self-belonging stands in stark contrast to the foundational question of the Heidelberg Catechism, "What is our only hope in life and death? That I am not my own, but belong—body and soul, in life and in death—to my faithful Savior, Jesus Christ."[1]

Elsewhere, Paul not only says you belong to God (1 Cor. 6:19–20), but presses us more into God's reality that "we all belong to each other" (Rom. 12:5 NLT).

Does this mean we all need to be cookie-cutter Christians? A chain of smiley, paper-doll people with coffee cups that contain out-of-context Bible verses? May it never be!

There is much about the sociological, gendered, philosophical, generational, and cultural breadth contained within the church that could be expressed, but let's stick to the immediate context. Whereas verse 4 starts with "There is one . . . ", verse 7 begins with "But to each one . . . ". It's here the notion of God's diverse, fearfully and wonderfully made children pushes against groupthink. God has graced each one in Christ with something unique. Is there maturity, trial/error, and working through how this functions practically? Absolutely. But this hearkens back to Ephesians 3, where the importance of manifold wisdom being displayed through the church comes into focus (Eph. 3:10–11).

For many of us, however, the hardest proposition in Ephesians 4:6 to hold onto isn't God being *over* all (because God is God), or even God *in* all (because who can discern the heart of a person?), but working *through* all. He works in all the in-between spaces where our inner lives intersect with each other, challenging, stretching, refining, and expanding what we thought the kingdom of God was all about. But God's church is built differently than other communities. Here's why: each Person of the Godhead is entirely themselves while giving honor to one another. There's also another subtle reason our passage gives us as to why the community of the church is different—our King is different.

Ephesians 4:7–10 is a riff on Psalm 68. Paul uses his creative imagination to bring a new Christ-centered interpretation to the ancient Psalm. In the original Psalm, it speaks of the imagery of a King *receiving* gifts, but as it's quoted here, it's the *giving* from the King to the people that is highlighted. The text pushes past the common truth of royal imagery to point to God's uncommon grace. While it is right and good to honor King Jesus, Christ isn't looking for attention or to have us fill some lack in him. Our King pours out blessings on his creation and kingdom. One of the ways he does that is by gifting a variety of leaders to his church.

THE SPACE BETWEEN US

I don't normally track my runs. I enjoy mapping out a 5k route through the city and then running it without any devices attached. Still, now and then, I'll carry my phone with the GPS app running to see my pace and completion time. A friend and I shared our running data a few years ago, and I plugged his pace in on my phone for my next run. Two things happened. First, I did not beat his pace. There are multiple reasons for this, such as age, build, and overall drive. Second, I ran my personal best. He, being himself, spurred me on to run my best.

There is so much unhealthy competition in the church today, whether between individuals, congregations, denominations, or leaders. This can stem from a lack of vision regarding the church's broad scope, or unresolved identity issues within ourselves. But if we are truly on the same team, a win, a personal best, a victory for one person is a victory for the whole. Just as teammates are called to push one another, despite having different strengths and positions, we are also called to spur one another on toward love and good deeds (Heb. 10:24–25).

Some of the gifts that Christ gives are people. These are men and women who help lead, not primarily in doing the work of the church, but in *equipping others* to minister and serve (v. 12).

> In ancient times, equipping had four different meanings: setting a broken bone correctly, packing a ship with supplies for a long journey, restoring something to its original condition, and preparing a soldier for battle. When leaders in the church begin to take seriously the call of equipping in their congregations [and city/regions], they begin to address issues of brokenness and healing in the world, they prepare others for the journey, and they help restore people to their original condition of shalom. They don't just give people truth; they also help them find ways to be strengthened for the battle ahead. [2]

Verse 11 raises many questions. Is this an exhaustive list? How do we define each of these roles? Are apostles and prophets roles for back then, but not now, or both now and then? Is it pastor *and* teacher or pastor-teacher? Those, and a dozen other questions, are good to work through. However, staying in the flow of our theme, a vital insight to notice is that there is a *plurality* of gifts given toward the *single* purpose of building up the church in unity, knowledge, and maturity in Christ (vv. 12–13).

Let's step back and evaluate our framework for spiritual growth. When we think of maturing, is our natural tendency to think about being "better" at prayer, or maybe having large sections of our Bible memorized and our theology perfect? Is it about how much we give or serve? Assuming we are coming from a place of what Christ has done for us first, all these things can be beneficial in our discipleship progress. But how much do we put time, thought, and practice into how we as a gospel *community* can only mature together? It is impossible to grow into the fullness of God without the interconnectivity of other believers. The interdependence called for in the body of Christ is mortifying, meaning that something within us often must die for new life to take place.

The supporting ligaments mentioned in verse 16 are needed resurrection ingredients. They represent the relationships we have among the body that support a growth regimen. Without joints to provide interdependence, many parts of the body simply don't function as they are designed to. Unfortunately, the picture that so many of our isolated religious communities represent is Christ's body dismembered and scattered throughout a city. Much like the community event mentioned at the opening of this chapter, all the parts are technically there, but they aren't working as one.

Part of the good news is that the Christ-centered people who are the church guard one another (v. 14). Gospel community protects from landmines and trip wires in the world that seek to destroy people's lives and faith. I have experienced more friends leaving the faith than I care to talk about. We all have doubts and need safe yet challenging places to explore, disagree, question, and reconstruct. I believe this is a natural part of following God (Ecclesiastes attests to this). Nevertheless, the place I, as a pastor, have seen "deconstruction" go downhill fast is when there is an abandonment of a local Christian community. That's when the waves of other ideas, philosophies, and desires not only rock the boat but capsize and shipwreck the life they had in Christ. However, the gifts of healthy leadership pointing to sound doctrine and a committed community showing the embodiment of doctrine, help to anchor us amid the chaos-waters.

In this first part of Ephesians 4, God reveals a beautiful landscape of the diversity and togetherness of the church. We must, however, guard against community and oneness becoming ends in themselves. A working body is essential, and it's also insufficient without Christ as its head. Paul will transition in Ephesians 4:17 to a discussion of identity and calling. An addendum of his words serves as a concluding thought for our current section: "So I tell you this, and insist on it in the Lord, that you must no longer live as the Gentiles do, in the futility of their thinking"—about the unity of the church.

PASTORAL ENCOURAGEMENT

I can't stress how vital non-staff, non-paid, lay Christians are in trying to get closer to the target of church unity. Leaders may be the pointed tip (and thank you!), but it's congregational buy-in and participation that enable the arrow to fly.

Another beautiful aspect of pursuing unity is that it not only blesses the church, but it also benefits the world. Jesus stresses in John 17:20−23 that when the world sees unity in the church, it's a witness to the world, a testimony that God sent his Son.

DISCUSSION QUESTIONS

1. Have you experienced disunity in the past, whether between church groups or individuals? In a posture of humility, how do you wish the interaction would have been different?

2. Do you recall any times when you were with a group of Christians you weren't close to and were surprised (in a good way!) with the interaction and experience?

3. In your city, what dividing lines are most prominent between churches? Ethnicity? Wealth? Denomination? Or something else?

4. Share a story about how an apostle, prophet, evangelist, pastor, or teacher has equipped you in some small way to embrace the kingdom of God.

5. In your social circles, are people more tempted toward staunch individualism or groupthink? Why do you think that is?

6. Thinking of God as Father, consider why it delights him for his children to work and play together.

7. Who are/were some of your closest Christian friends from other congregations? What do you enjoy about them and their faith?

SPIRITUAL PRACTICES TO CONSIDER
FOR EPHESIANS 4:1–16

❖ **Pray Palms Down / Palms Up:** In quiet reflection, bring before the Lord the times "the church" or another Christian has hurt or offended you. With your hands open, palms facing down, imagine the different hurts and bitterness falling away. Then, with palms up, ask the Holy Spirit to speak to you words of healing and pursuit in forgiving and blessing or reconciling with that situation.

❖ **Confession:** Take a moment to survey your life and reflect on where you haven't made every effort to pursue the unity of the saints. Write to God a short letter of confession and repentance, acknowledging your confusion, misunderstanding, or downright wrongness in speaking or doing ill to the body of Christ.

❖ **Pilgrimage:** Take the time to plan out how your schedule and commitment may allow for you (or a group) to worship with other congregations. In a posture of curiosity rather than criticism, take a step in fellowshipping and praising alongside another part of the body of Christ on "their turf."

9

Created to Be Like God

Ruth Martin

EPHESIANS 4:17–32

¹⁷ So I tell you this, and insist on it in the Lord, that you must no longer live as the Gentiles do, in the futility of their thinking. ¹⁸ They are darkened in their understanding and separated from the life of God because of the ignorance that is in them due to the hardening of their hearts. ¹⁹ Having lost all sensitivity, they have given themselves over to sensuality so as to indulge in every kind of impurity, and they are full of greed.

²⁰ That, however, is not the way of life you learned ²¹ when you heard about Christ and were taught in him in accordance with the truth that is in Jesus. ²² You were taught, with regard to your former way of life, to put off your old self, which is being corrupted by its deceitful desires; ²³ to be made new in the attitude of your minds; ²⁴ and to put on the new self, created to be like God in true righteousness and holiness.

²⁵ Therefore each of you must put off falsehood and speak truthfully to your neighbor, for we are all members of one body. ²⁶ "In your anger do not sin": Do not let the sun go down while you are still angry, ²⁷ and do not give the devil a foothold. ²⁸ Anyone who has been stealing must steal no longer, but must work, doing something useful with their own hands, that they may have something to share with those in need.

²⁹ Do not let any unwholesome talk come out of your mouths, but only what is helpful for building others up ac-

cording to their needs, that it may benefit those who listen. [30] And do not grieve the Holy Spirit of God, with whom you were sealed for the day of redemption. [31] Get rid of all bitterness, rage and anger, brawling and slander, along with every form of malice. [32] Be kind and compassionate to one another, forgiving each other, just as in Christ God forgave you.

LEARNING HOW TO BE SOMETHING NEW

JLOVE BEING AN AUNT.

These are words I never imagined saying. In fact, I used to think people who were obsessed with their nieces and nephews were "crazy aunts/uncles." But now I get it. I have a niece and a nephew, with another nephew on the way, and I am unashamedly obsessed with these kiddos.

As a crazy aunt, I now routinely wake up at 5 a.m. on a Saturday morning to drive four hours for my niece's 9 a.m. soccer game that lasts a mere forty-five minutes. My niece Aria is four years old, and this is her first time competing on a sports team. As one of the youngest players, she is just beginning to learn the rudimentary basics of soccer. Soccer involves a lot of running, but it is not *only* about running. Soccer involves kicking a ball, but it's also not *just* kicking a ball. Aria is learning about passing the ball, moving the ball toward one goal and away from the other, not touching the ball with her hands, and other basic soccer rules.

Though I never played high school sports, my siblings were involved in many years of soccer, so even as a spectator, I have learned the rules of how to play the game. Although I never wore a team jersey, I understand the roles of the various positions. Aria does wear a team jersey, but all the information is new to her. She does not yet fully understand the game. She is learning that being a soccer player comes with specific roles and rules, behaviors that differ from just being a kid who likes to run. Aria has entered something bigger than herself—she can't just do whatever she wants. She is learning how to be a soccer player—a part of a team playing a specific game. When we enter life in Christ, and step onto the field of play he has designed, we are like a young soccer player needing to learn the rules of the game, and the specific role the Spirit intends for us to play within our new way of living.

THIS GOES FOR YOU TOO

After three rich chapters establishing a theological understanding of the Ephesians's identity in Christ and full membership in God's family, Paul begins to instruct the Ephesians about the practicalities of what life looks like as Christians. It can be easy to read this latter half of the letter to the Ephesians as a list of dos and don'ts. "This action is bad; this one is good." But Paul is not simply making a moralistic to-do list. He is describing two fundamentally different identities, two ways of life.

There is the way of decay (Paul calls this the way "Gentiles" live, or the "old self," or "the flesh") and the way of new creation (the "new self"). "Decay" captures the progression over time of a life in opposition toward God, a life that progresses toward death. If Paul is using the imagery of "building up" the body, "decay" portrays the opposite: a life that is wasting away and becoming lifeless. This "way of decay" involves a crusting over of the heart, where the conscience is unresponsive to God's Spirit. Paul writes that the Ephesian Christians were living in the way of decay before they became followers of Jesus. In writing about our consciences, F. F. Bruce says the "habitual ignoring of the warning signals [the conscience] sends out incapacitates it from fulfilling its proper function."[1] Lives that have ignored the conviction of the Spirit calling to the conscience will have a warped view of wrongdoing. These lives have a certain quality; there are signs that mark this way of decay. This is how the Ephesians used to live—ignorant of God as seen in their patterns of selfishness and pride.

The city of Ephesus was a major trade hub in the Roman empire, and the Greek goddess of Artemis was the chief deity, with many large temples dedicated to her throughout Ephesus. Much of the Ephesian culture was centered on this goddess. New Testament scholar Clinton E. Arnold states the relationship between Artemis and Ephesus was "forged in terms of a divinely directed covenant relationship."[2] Though the Artemis cult dominated the city, Ephesus also worshiped other deities, including a few from Egypt. The religious culture in Ephesus could be described as pluralistic and polytheistic. Magical practices were prevalent, with the assumption that "good and evil spirits were involved in practically every area of life."[3] This paganism of Ephesus is the way of decay, and Paul recognizes that the Ephesian believers were once such pagans.

But the Ephesians who have come into relationship with Jesus are no longer people of death and decay. They are in Christ. As Paul writes in verses 20 and 21 (ESV), the Ephesian believers have "learned Christ" and "heard about him and were taught in him." Because the Greek text does not have a preposition after "heard," a more word-for-word translation would be "you have heard him." Thus, even though other Christians were the ones doing the teaching about Christ (Acts 18:19–26 says Priscilla, Aquila, and Apollos were Christian leaders in Ephesus), in a deeper sense it was the voice of Jesus himself whom they heard. John Stott explains that verses 20–21 communicate,

Christ is himself the substance of Christian teaching . . . is himself also the teacher . . . was also the context, even the atmosphere within which the teaching was given. When Jesus Christ is at once the subject, the object and the environment of the moral instruction being given, we may have confidence that it is truly Christian. For *truth is in Jesus.*[4]

The truth is that the Ephesian believers are a new creation and are now members of his body—the church. God has made a new humanity, a people who are called to be set apart and to live rightly in relationship to God and with others. The new identity is not simply the reverse image of the way of decay. No, the new creation life looks like Jesus, because the church is his body. The Spirit has been, is now, and will continue building up the body of Christ until she matures into full resemblance of Jesus. Therefore, the old patterns of decay must go. As members of Jesus' body, believers are to express, through their behaviors, the traits of Christ himself.

For four-year-olds learning soccer, the behaviors they're used to at home (picking up the ball with their hands or running and kicking aimlessly) need to change. "No, you can't pick up the ball. No, this is the wrong goal you are heading toward." The kids need to be instructed in what being a soccer player entails. The same goes for people who were once ignorant of Jesus and his ways; we need to be instructed in what being a follower of Jesus means for our lives. Paul is instructing Christians to look at Jesus and model our lives after him. Paul provides specific directions in what this looks like.

Lest we lose sight of the larger picture of Ephesians 4, keep in mind that Paul's concern is about the unity of the body of Christ (v. 4:3). He is drawing our attention to the body reaching full maturity—the whole church growing up together in Christ (v. 4:13). Our lives as Christians are more than our own personal freedoms or individual choices. "You do you" is not a motto for Christians to embody. The song "I Need You to Survive" by Hezekiah Walker is a more accurate statement of life together as believers: it speaks of our mutual need for each other in order to survive as part of the body of Christ. Our behaviors impact each other, even beyond our households! We are members of one body, and so the behaviors of the new creation life can only be understood within this context of one unified body comprised of many parts.

Though the NIV translates verse 25 as "each of you must put off falsehood and speak truthfully to your neighbor," the Greek text has *plural* forms of the verbs. Paul is addressing the corporate body of Ephesians believers: his imperatives are for all the believers to hear and obey. The following imperatives change to singular forms, zeroing in on the importance of every believer to take heed. The imperatives are both/and. As corporate bodies of believers, his imperatives are for us to obey. As individual members, his words are a standard for our lives too.

LET'S DO THIS

In Ephesians 4:25, Paul gets into the practical details of this way of new creation. Though he will cover more areas of life in chapters 5 and 6, here in the remaining part of chapter 4 Paul highlights our words, our anger, our possessions, and our conduct toward each other. He both describes what *not* to do and what believers *should* do. These ethical imperatives are not ends in and of themselves. They chart a path of living in line with Christ, a path that draws us toward him and makes us more like him. Eugene Peterson calls the prohibitions "negative space" that work to counter . . .

actions and attitudes that were accepted as commonplace, some even sanctioned, in the Gentile culture of
Ephesians . . . As we immerse ourselves in church, we realize that there are culturally accepted practices, Gentile
ways of life, that we must set aside. [5]

The prohibitions are a description of the way of decay. Lying
and deception, letting anger control us, greed and stealing, and
words that hinder unity are all markers of the old way. These
are not the patterns of Jesus, and neither should they be the
patterns of his body. If the members of the body are living in the
ways of decay, the whole body cannot grow toward healthy maturity. On the contrary, the positive imperatives call believers to
live like Christ in our relationships: speaking the truth, rightly
handling anger, living generously, speaking life-giving words,
and reflecting God's kindness, compassion, and forgiveness.
These are signs of a body growing into the maturity of Christ.
How we live and treat each other affects who we become.

If I were to walk around my neighborhood and come across
a kid in her yard bouncing a ball on her feet or hitting the ball
with her head, I would guess she is a soccer player practicing
soccer drills. On the flip side, if I knew someone who was on a
soccer team, but they never practiced (either on their own or as
part of team practices), I would assume they are not actually
serious about playing soccer at a higher level. As followers of
Jesus, our individual lives should show patterns and behaviors
that mirror his own. Our churches should show signs that we
are living as a new creation as a body.

I believe our churches should be the prime examples of
where healthy communicating of truth occurs, in ways that
humbly build up one another. We may talk highly of generosity, but generosity is something to live out, not just in words
but in action. Examine the relationships between our churches.

May our words spoken about these congregations be words that bless rather than words that demean those churches, revealing a spirit of envy or pride within our midst.

Because God's heart is for the church to pursue unity, we grieve his Spirit when our words and attitudes cut down other parts of his body. We must be sensitive—not callous—to how God wants us to relate to other churches. Our postures and behaviors, corporately and individually, are to be consistent with the new creation life in Christ. In the areas where we exhibit the old way of decay, repentance and submission to Christ is needed.

PASTORAL ENCOURAGEMENT

My encouragement is not to approach this section of Ephesians as a to-do list, as a way to level-up as a Christian. Dig into how these imperatives to Christians connect us to Jesus. Go over Paul's imperatives and connect them to where we see Jesus in the four Gospels embodying these qualities. Ponder the instances when anger, greed, and improper words would be the typical human response yet when Jesus was kind, tenderhearted, and forgiving.

Jesus has shown us how to live and has given us the Holy Spirit to empower us to live rightly. May our desire increase to become more like him. Pray and ask God to help you in these areas Paul writes about. Consider asking the people closest to you to help you in these areas.

DISCUSSION QUESTIONS

1. What are experiences you've had in needing to learn new behaviors or traits, a new way of "being"?

2. What does it mean to have Christ as the "standard"? How do we actually model our lives after him?

3. List some areas where Christ's transformation in your life has been difficult to learn. How do you see growth toward his maturity in your life?

4. Where is your church growing in reflecting Christ's character? Are there aspects God might be highlighting that are in need of maturing? Consider these questions especially in relation to the other churches in your area.

5. What relationships come to mind as you read Paul's imperatives? Are there relationships that bring out of you a cutting spirit? Pray for the Holy Spirit's conviction as you interact with those relationships; ask the Spirit to teach you how to love these people.

SPIRITUAL PRACTICES TO CONSIDER
FOR EPHESIANS4:17–32

❖ **Examen:** The Ignatian practice of Examen is a way to reflect on a period of time, usually one day.[6] In this practice of prayerful reflection, we look over our day to notice how God was present, when we might have been walking in step with the Spirit and when we were not.

> ✦ Set aside twenty minutes at the end of your day. You can do the Examen through journaling or conversing with another person or simply being still and silently reflecting. Take a minute to breathe and quiet yourself.
>
> ✦ What parts of your day are you grateful for? Give God thanks for these parts.
>
> ✦ What are the things that led you toward God today? What are the things that led you away from God?
>
> ✦ When did you have the greatest sense of leaning into the way of new creation?
>
> ✦ When did you have a sense of leaning into the way of decay?
>
> ✦ Humbly ask God if he has an invitation for you as you reflect on the day's events.
>
> ✦ As you think about the next day, offer tomorrow to God in surrender.

❖ **Faults and Affirmations:** I came across this practice in *Finding Freedom in Constraint* by Jared Boyd.[7] While the Examen practice can be done individually, Faults and Affirmations is to be done with others. This practice is a way of speaking the truth to one another. In the "faults" portion, we confess the truth about places of sin in our life in the vein of James 5:16 ("Confess your sins to each other and pray for each other so that you may be healed"). In the "affirmations" portion, we speak the truth to the other members of Christ's body in a way that builds up and encourages us toward growth in Christ.

+ Once you have another person or a group of people on board with doing this practice, begin by sharing a fault that is appropriate to share within the context of these relationships. (For example, "I confess that I spent more money than I intended to today, money I had intended on giving to a Christian ministry.")

+ If you are hearing someone confess a fault, consider extending forgiveness to this sibling in Christ. Boyd writes that forgiveness is "something we need to practice just like we practice learning an instrument or making an omelet."[8]

+ Speak a true affirmation to one another. What is something good you notice in the person in front of you? See and name God's goodness evident in the life of this member of Jesus' body. This might be related to a task they've done well, or it might be about character traits that reflect Jesus.

10

Children of the Light

Matt DeMontaigne, Jen Meter, & Chris M. Slawecki

EPHESIANS 5:1–20

[1] Follow God's example, therefore, as dearly loved children [2] and walk in the way of love, just as Christ loved us and gave himself up for us as a fragrant offering and sacrifice to God.

[3] But among you there must not be even a hint of sexual immorality, or of any kind of impurity, or of greed, because these are improper for God's holy people. [4] Nor should there be obscenity, foolish talk or coarse joking, which are out of place, but rather thanksgiving. [5] For of this you can be sure: No immoral, impure or greedy person—such a person is an idolater—has any inheritance in the kingdom of Christ and of God. [6] Let no one deceive you with empty words, for because of such things God's wrath comes on those who are disobedient. [7] Therefore do not be partners with them.

[8] For you were once darkness, but now you are light in the Lord. Live as children of light [9] (for the fruit of the light consists in all goodness, righteousness and truth) [10] and find out what pleases the Lord. [11] Have nothing to do with the fruitless deeds of darkness, but rather expose them. [12] It is shameful even to mention what the disobedient do in secret. [13] But everything

exposed by the light becomes visible—and everything that is illuminated becomes a light. [14] This is why it is said:

"Wake up, sleeper,
    rise from the dead,
        and Christ will shine on you."

[15] Be very careful, then, how you live—not as unwise but as wise, [16] making the most of every opportunity, because the days are evil. [17] Therefore do not be foolish, but understand what the Lord's will is. [18] Do not get drunk on wine, which leads to debauchery. Instead, be filled with the Spirit, [19] speaking to one another with psalms, hymns, and songs from the Spirit. Sing and make music from your heart to the Lord, [20] always giving thanks to God the Father for everything, in the name of our Lord Jesus Christ.

FOR YOU WERE ONCE DARKNESS

DO YOU REMEMBER BEING A child and closing your eyes, pretending to be blind? Walking around, hands outstretched, bumping into furniture while imagining what it would be like to live in total darkness? Then every once in a while, you'd squint one eye open to make sure you could still see—make sure you could escape the darkness.

Darkness can be scary. Sight is fundamentally the process of gathering reflections of light around us. So, if there is no light—there is no sight! Darkness makes it easier for us to stub a toe. Or for someone to sneak up on us. Darkness makes us feel vulnerable. It increases our fear of the unknown and evokes feelings of loneliness, sadness, and depression.

The very first chapter of the Bible begins with the earth in a state of complete darkness. God's first creative act is to speak light into existence:

> And God said, "Let there be light," and there was light.
> God saw that the light was good, and he separated the
> light from the darkness. (Gen. 1:3–4)

In addition to the absence of light and sight, darkness is also often a symbol for the absence of God. The dark provides cover for those who wish to engage in unethical or sinful behaviors. The Bible frequently associates darkness with evil deeds and moral depravity.

Paul draws upon these themes as he reminds the Ephesian church "you were once darkness" (v. 8). The Ephesians were no strangers to the dark. They were living in a culture filled with both spiritual and corporeal difficulties. Remember what Paul referenced one chapter earlier in Ephesians? In Ephesians 4, he identifies a variety of ways that darkness seems to have invaded the church of Ephesus—through lying, sexual immorality, stealing, greed, and vulgar speech. Now, in chapter 5, he repeats many of these same themes again, reminding the church that actions done in secret—in the dark—will keep us in spiritual darkness as well.

Paul does not shy away from naming the vices that are offensive and contradictory to the way of Jesus. He explains that those who stay in the dark will not have "any inheritance in the kingdom of Christ and of God" (v. 5). This could very much seem like an ominous warning: *"Listen, church: You better knock it off and straighten up or you're gonna lose your inheritance!"*

However, in the context of Ephesians (and all of Scripture), this does not seem to align with the truth: "by grace you have been saved, through faith . . . not by works" (Eph. 2:8–9). If salvation is by grace alone, how can we lose it? Is Paul now saying that our inheritance is earned by our good deeds? This would make no sense at all!

No. Paul is not threatening people with a work-for-your-salvation ultimatum. The reality is we all sin. Many of us have struggled (and still struggle!) with some of the sins he lists. But when we put our faith in Jesus, these things no longer *define* us. We have a new identity: children of the light. But we cannot walk in the light if we keep our sins hidden! To follow Jesus means to confront darkness head-on with the light of the gospel. Paul then shows us the way to do that.

THE HINGE OF FORGIVENESS

Between these two lists of "dark deeds" in chapters 4 and 5, there is a "hinge"—a means by which Paul encourages the church to take hold of their identity as children of the light. How can we "put off the old self" mentioned in chapter 4 and "live as children of light" as he describes it in chapter 5? Paul's answer to this question is we are to "follow God's example." Other translations say, "be imitators of God." This imitation begins with Christ's example of forgiveness: "[forgive] each other, just as in Christ God forgave you" (Eph. 4:32).

The transformation of darkness to light must happen from the inside out, and it always begins with our receiving God's forgiveness first. This entire spiritual metamorphosis begins with the grace of Jesus Christ, which is accessed through his forgiveness. When we step into the forgiveness that Jesus offers freely, we are rescued out of the kingdom of darkness and brought into the kingdom of light. Forgiveness is the hinge that swings the door wide between these two realms. This is exactly what Paul says in Colossians 1 when he writes, "For he has rescued us from the dominion of darkness and brought us into the kingdom of the Son he loves, in whom we have redemption, the forgiveness of sins" (Col. 1:13–14).

Because we have been forgiven—we forgive each other! This is a major theme of Paul's teaching. It comes up repeatedly throughout his letters. Whenever Paul writes this, he does so confidently, knowing he is echoing the very heart of Christ. Jesus says in Matthew 6, "For if you forgive other people when they sin against you, your heavenly Father will also forgive you. But if you do not forgive others their sins, your Father will not forgive your sins" (Matt. 6:14–15).

The door between the kingdom of darkness and the kingdom of light is opened to us by the grace of Jesus—and the hinge holding it all together is *forgiveness*. Every time we forgive someone else, we allow the door to swing wide into the mystery of grace, giving those around us—as well as ourselves—a better view of the kingdom of light.

WALK IN THE WAY OF LOVE

Paul reminds the church they are not simply fleeing darkness, but they *were* darkness that has been *transformed* by the light of Christ. Paul is very clear that we are not just *in* the light, but WE ARE THE LIGHT itself. If we are imitators of God, and he is the source of light, then our lives cannot help but reflect this same light. And what is the primary way we reflect him? By living in his love. Paul writes, "And walk in the way of love, just as Christ loved us and gave himself up for us as a fragrant offering and sacrifice to God" (Eph. 5:2).

However, the actions Paul has been listing display a disordered kind of love: sexual immorality, impurity, and obscenity. This is the type of love that exists in darkness. For example, the world often interchanges the concept of love with sexual acts. The phrase "making love" immediately suggests two people having sex because the world has often diminished the idea of love to a singular physical act. And often this act is highly self-focused and self-gratifying—rather than imitating the sacrificial and grace-filled love of Christ.

If we are imitators of God—children of the light—then we must imitate the self-sacrificial love of Jesus, who suffered and embraced death on the cross in order to give us abundant life. Just as children learn from parents' example, as we follow Christ, we will "walk in the way of love."

THE TRANSFORMING POWER OF LIGHT

After compelling us to transform darkness into light as we imitate God (primarily through forgiveness and love), Paul then explains, "everything exposed by the light becomes visible"—then takes it a step further and says, "and everything that is illuminated **becomes** a light."

We know the shame and secrecy that comes with living in darkness—but light changes everything! Paul is saying once sin is uncovered and made visible (because of the light), it loses its power of concealment and is transformed into light itself! It becomes open, apparent, and undisguised. Exposure to light strips away sin's ability to remain hidden in the dark. Instead, it stands in the open realm of truth and accountability—which is the nature of light. As the kids' say . . . it's lit!

However, how we "expose" darkness is of critical importance here. In no way is Paul building an "exposure police force"! Remember—we had just been instructed to forgive and love. In no way should we twist this into some kind of commandment to judge, where we feel obligated to call out others' sin (or even worse—find pleasure in it) to make ourselves feel better. Judging and comparing others' behavior to our own catches us in the evil one's devious plot, too.

Paul's instruction here does not mean we should not love those in darkness. Jesus hung out with sinners all the time! The impure, the greedy, the sexually deviant—Jesus came to seek and save the lost. We are to not abandon people caught in the struggle of darkness.

So, then, how do we go about "exposing" sin? Instead of judgment upon those walking in darkness, Paul offers a simple solution: "Live as children of light (for the fruit of the light consists in all goodness, righteousness and truth)" (vv. 8–9). **We expose the darkness simply by living in the light.** Paul seems to be echoing Jesus' words in the Gospel of Matthew:

> You are the light of the world. A town built on a hill cannot be hidden. Neither do people light a lamp and put it under a bowl. Instead, they put it on its stand, and it gives light to everyone in the house. In the same way, let your light shine before others, that they may see your good deeds and glorify your Father in heaven. (Matt. 5:14–16)

Jesus does *not* say "Let your light shine by publicly declaring everyone's sins, greediness, impurities, and vulgar speech, so they may see how awesome you are." Instead, we can be confident any fruit—any goodness, righteousness, and truthfulness—that flows out from us will be our testimony to the light of Christ in our lives. This is what will light up the world around us, revealing there is a different way—a different kingdom—and in the process, transform the darkness into light.

A FEW PRACTICAL EXAMPLES

Paul then goes on to give a few key helpful examples of the transforming power of light. The first is in verse 17—instead of being foolish, we should understand the will of the Lord. Paul is returning to the renewal of the mind he had mentioned in Ephesians 4:23. Be wise. Don't be foolish. Spend your time and energy discerning the will of the Lord over and above anything else.

He then moves on to an example of something that will most likely infringe on one's mental capacity: drinking too much wine. Verses 18–19 suggest replacing a filling of wine with a filling of the Holy Spirit. Drinking too much wine will certainly distort our ability to think with wisdom and discern the will of the Lord. This fact has been proven throughout man's history, both publicly and privately. Instead of wine, children of the light are to be filled with the Spirit of God. While we are guaranteed the seal of the Spirit upon placing our faith in Christ (Eph. 1:13–14), Paul seems to be speaking to a different work of the Spirit here. He is speaking not just of a one-time event— but an ongoing, continual act as we walk with Jesus. When we present ourselves as vessels to God for him to use—he will most certainly fill us up—and spill over!

Another example of the transforming power of light is that this filling of the Spirit is often fleshed out through "psalms, hymns, and songs from the Spirit." Here at Valley View Community Church, we absolutely love to worship. We value it and see how God utilizes worship in song to change our lives. Paul encourages the Ephesian church to praise God through songs— songs to one another (which build up the body of Christ), and songs to the Lord (which bless and praise the triune God).

Paul seamlessly transitions from worship to thanksgiving, as another example of the transforming power of light—"giving thanks to God the Father for everything, in the name of our Lord Jesus Christ." We have an all-encompassing worship—not just when things are good, but when things are not so good as well. When we remain in a place of gratitude, we are aligning with the new, redeemed nature of our identity as imitators of God and children of light. Thanksgiving represents the kind of edifying, grace-filled heart that should characterize God's people. Thankfulness keeps us centered on Christ and submitted to his will for our lives.

We all live in two worlds at once: the world as it is, with all its brokenness and darkness—but also the world that is being transformed by the glory and light of Jesus Christ. And you are part of that transformation. You are the light.

PASTORAL ENCOURAGEMENT

If you are "in Christ" then you are in the light. Paul is very clear that we have the light of the Lord in us. **You are light.** You are no longer darkness. Paul encourages us to walk as children of the light, to be the fruit of light, be goodness, be righteousness, be truthful. He then returned to the concept of renewing the Spirit of the mind, of seeking what is pleasing to the Lord. With all this darkness around, you must chase after what pleases the Lord. Amplify that light to everyone around you.

DISCUSSION QUESTIONS

1. Do you ever feel more like a child of darkness than a child of the light? If so, how might God be calling you to embrace your true identity?

2. Does your life demonstrate the "fruit of light" (Paul offers the examples of goodness, righteousness, and truthfulness)? If not, perhaps you might consider spending some time examining the "hinge" of forgiveness—is there an area you need to receive God's forgiveness? Are you harboring unforgiveness in your heart toward someone?

3. Are you sometimes tempted to expose others' sins rather than expose and confess your own?

4. How might God be calling you to shine his light this week?

SPIRITUAL PRACTICES TO CONSIDER
FOR EPHESIANS 5:1–20

❖ **Confession.** Is there an area of your life where the Lord might be inviting you to expose darkness, confess your sin, and be healed (James 5:16)? While confessing to Jesus is crucial, confessing to a fellow brother or sister in Christ is also important. Pray about who the Holy Spirit might have you confess to in order to bring your darkness into the light.

❖ **Make a List of the Transforming Work of the Spirit.** Ask the Holy Spirit to highlight areas of your life where he has demonstrated his transforming power and make a list. Continue to add to this list as he continues to do his transforming work in your life.

❖ **Gratitude.** Spend some time in a spirit of gratitude, thanking the Lord for everything he has done for you!

11

𝕬 𝕾𝖕𝖎𝖗𝖎𝖙-𝕱𝖎𝖑𝖑𝖊𝖉 𝕸𝖆𝖗𝖗𝖎𝖆𝖌𝖊

Matt DeMontaigne, Jen Meter,
& Chris M. Slawecki

EPHESIANS 5:21–33

[21] Submit to one another out of reverence for Christ.

[22] Wives, submit yourselves to your own husbands as you do to the Lord. [23] For the husband is the head of the wife as Christ is the head of the church, his body, of which he is the Savior.[24] Now as the church submits to Christ, so also wives should submit to their husbands in everything.

[25] Husbands, love your wives, just as Christ loved the church and gave himself up for her [26] to make her holy, cleansing her by the washing with water through the word, [27] and to present her to himself as a radiant church, without stain or wrinkle or any other blemish, but holy and blameless. [28] In this same way, husbands ought to love their wives as their own bodies. He who loves his wife loves himself. [29] After all, no one ever hated their own body, but they feed and care for their body, just as Christ does the church— [30] for we are members of his body. [31] "For this reason a man will leave his father and mother and be united to his wife, and the two will become one flesh." [32] This is a profound mystery—but I am talking about Christ and the church. [33] However, each one of you also must love his wife as he loves himself, and the wife must respect her husband.

GRATEFUL SUBMISSION

WHAT DO YOU THINK OF when you hear the word "submit"? For many of us, there may be an immediate negative connotation as our minds conjure up thoughts of enforced obedience, slavery, government dictators, and police brutality.

So, when we read the words Paul begins this section with, "Submit to one another," we must be careful to guard against those images and be willing to re-frame our concept of submission. Let's keep in mind this verse does not appear out of thin air. It is linked to the previous verse (v. 20), where we are exhorted to "always [give] thanks to God the Father for everything." A heart that is grateful is a heart that is submitted to Christ because it acknowledges God is the source of all good gifts. As we give thanks for the grace, salvation, and provisions God bestows upon us, our heart moves away from self-idolatry—and focuses instead on our Creator.

MUTUAL SUBMISSION

Although modern readers may balk a bit at the entire concept of submission, to Paul's readers, submission was a cultural norm. But what would have been radically countercultural to them at the time of their reading this letter, was the idea of *mutual* submission.

This first phrase sets the tone for all relationships among believers. Mutual submission is an attitude of deference, love, and service toward one another—and it's the opposite of the greed, immorality, and self-gratification Paul had just warned us about. Paul is calling Christians to counter the selfish and self-promoting attitudes of the world with the Christ-like humility that is willing to suffer and sacrifice for the other.

RE-FRAMING SUBMISSION

Unfortunately, this term and its meaning have led to all kinds of misconstrued interpretations of what Paul is talking about, especially regarding wives submitting to husbands. People have placed a hyper-focus on one section of the verse without considering the context of the entire passage.

What then, in the full context of what Paul is teaching, does "submit" mean?

In its simplest form, *to submit* means *to place* or *arrange under*. The Greek-English lexicon tells us that submission is "voluntarily yielding in love." Many commentators note submission is willingly following someone else's leadership. So, there is a relational subjecting of oneself to another, but it is not in a subservient, "superior vs. inferior," caste-creating kind of way. It is instead a voluntary willingness to give of oneself, motivated by love, in service to the other.

Paul says we submit to one another *out of reverence for Christ*. We do this because this is the way of Jesus. This is not the only place Christians are instructed to act in a humble, sacrificial way. Galatians 5:13 tells us to "serve one another humbly in love." And in Philippians 2:3–4, we are encouraged to "do nothing out of selfish ambition or vain conceit. Rather, in humility value others above yourselves, not looking to your own interests but each of you to the interests of the others."

This is what Christ modeled for his church in *all* relationships, including the marriage relationship: mutually yielding to one another in love.

SOME HISTORICAL CONTEXT

As we read these Spirit-enlightened words written by Paul, we must acknowledge the cultural context Paul and these early

Christians lived in. Paul had to be wise as he laid these "house codes" out, so as not to stir the pot too much. Remember, he was already in jail, and he was writing in a time when the roles within marriage and culture itself were vastly different than what we see today. And, because Rome was suspicious that minority religious groups were undermining traditional values, these groups often labored to reassure the authorities their beliefs fit within the framework of Roman values.

Have you ever heard of "house codes"? In ancient Greece and then subsequently in Rome, various philosophers, writers, and politicians published their own versions of what they imagined family and societal structure should look like. Aristotle had a version he published, as did many other leaders and thinkers. In each prominent version of these house codes society was structured like a pyramid. At the top were free, educated men called the "paterfamilias." Then, under the head of the household were the various other groups. The lower on the pyramid, the lower in value a person was considered. You did not want to be a slave, lower-class woman, or impoverished child. Can you imagine what life must have been like if you were a young, female slave?

Early Christians proclaimed a radical new teaching—all people were equal in value, loved by God, and welcomed into the family of Christ. Paul even began to call Christian slaves the spiritual equals of their owners (see the letter to Philemon). Can you picture how radical and subversive teachings like that must have seemed to first century Romans—especially to paterfamilias!

Early Christians had a delicate tightrope to walk. They believed all people were worthy of love, but they constituted a tiny minority in the vast sea of the Roman Empire. Early Christians were being pressured by Jewish leaders to become much more culturally Jewish and simultaneously by Roman authorities to stop stirring up so much trouble. Here it is worth quoting at length from New Testament theologian Klyne Snodgrass. He writes,

> "House Codes" is the label assigned to those sections of Ephesians, Colossians, and 1 Peter that give instructions to wives and husbands, children and parents, and slaves and masters. While these same three relationships were frequently addressed by Greek and Jewish writers in somewhat stereotypical fashion, no source for the Christian house codes has been discovered, nor do Greek or Jewish writers use the same language as the New Testament writers. The specific wording of this material emerged within the church.
>
> Christians had to treat these subjects, at least in part, because they were accused of destroying society with their focus on freedom, love, and following Christ. Non-Christians needed to know that this was not the case, and Christians needed to be taught the relevance of their faith for their primary social relations. Unlike other house codes, Christian house codes focused not only on wives, children, and slaves, but also on the responsibilities of the more powerful persons (husbands, parents, and masters). [1]

Returning to Ephesians 5, we can see how Paul intentionally begins this section by acknowledging the cultural norm—submission—but then he adds something distinctly Christian to it—submit *to one another*. Paul then goes on to offer thoughts concerning the house codes in three different relationships—husbands and wives, children and parents, and slaves and masters—but since the rest of Ephesians 5 deals only with wives and husbands, that is our focus for the rest of this discussion.

WIVES ... SUBMIT AS TO THE LORD

After he sets the overall tone for relationships, Paul then specifically addresses mutual submission in husbands and wives. For
wives, this means submitting to their husbands *as to the Lord*
(echoing the verse prior: "out of reverence for Christ").

Now this is a notoriously difficult passage to fully understand. In the NIV, as with many English translations, the English word *submit* is added into verse 22. So, in the NIV the
verse reads, "Wives, submit yourselves to your own husbands
as you do to the Lord." However, in the Greek text, the word
submit is not there. *Submit* appears in verse 21 but not 22 in
Greek. Instead, it is a continuation of the previous statement.
So, a more literal (but awkward in English) translation would
be something like: "Submit to one another out of reverence for
Christ. Wives to your husbands as to the Lord."

Snodgrass writes,

> Verse 23 is surely one of the most abused and debated
> texts in the New Testament. Its focus is not on the priv-
> ilege and dominance of the husband, and Paul never in-
> tended to suggest that wives were servants, compelled
> to follow any and every desire of the husband. The text
> does not tell women to obey their husbands, nor does it
> give any license for husbands to attempt to force submis-
> sion. [2]

For the women reading Paul's letter, there was no option to
not submit. The entire society was fashioned so that they had
little power. But Paul here is spiritually *empowering* wives by
reminding them that although they cannot control their situation, they can control the posture of their hearts. *How* and *why*
they submit is what demonstrates their reverence to Christ.
Regardless of whether their husband was kind or cruel, understanding or belittling, affectionate or abusive ... they could sub-

mit to him *as if they were submitting to the Lord*. And the Lord their God would "see their heart" (1 Sam. 16:7) and reward what is done in secret (Matt. 6:4).

While this would have been incredibly difficult for wives to live this out in Paul's day, it is still a real challenge for many of us today. Mutual submission is not easy—for women or men. A woman I once counseled was struggling to forgive her husband for some choices he made that brought much pain and trauma into their marriage and home. She knew God had called her to forgive him, but this was not something that would come naturally or easily! However, *because of her reverence for Christ,* and because she wanted to imitate him, she willingly submitted herself to her husband. And in the forgiveness, she found freedom. Not freedom from pain or unhappiness—who among us could ever escape that in this world? What she found was freedom from being bound and embittered.

HUSBANDS ... LOVE AS CHRIST

Paul then shifts his attention to those with cultural power (the men) and gives the first of two metaphors to help explain this mutual submission further: "Husbands, love your wives, just as Christ loved the church and gave himself up for her."

Then he offers a second metaphor that parallels the first: "In this same way, husbands ought to love their wives as their own bodies." So, husbands should love their wives the way Christ loves the church and the way they love their own bodies.

Both metaphors demonstrate sacrificial and mutual submission. Christ "gave himself up" for the church, suffering a gruesome death, so we might have abundant life. And when our body requires attention, it is difficult to ignore it! Even the smallest wound on our body demands we submit to its needs—a blister requires a bandage, a pulled muscle requires rest until it heals. In this way, Paul is reminding husbands to consider their wives' needs and be willing to submit to them as they follow Christ's example of loving sacrifice.

Unfortunately, church history is filled with examples of spiritual leaders abusing power. So much church hurt is a result of hypocrisy and misuse of authority by those God called to be servants. Much of the carnage and misinterpretation of what defines real power has been derived from a misreading of this passage, particularly verse 23: "For the husband is the head of the wife as Christ is the head of the church, his body."

The Greek word for "head" used here is *kephale*. This is the part of the body that holds the brain. When we interpret this word through our modern understanding and the English language, it seems to relate almost exclusively to leadership and/or authority, which then leads to the conclusion that men have authority over women, or men should lead women. This makes sense particularly in our modern, technological era. We tend to think of people's brains as the computer that controls them. Not so in Paul's worldview.

The word *kephale* is also interpreted as *being the source of*. For example, Paul writes earlier in Ephesians 4:15–16,

> Instead, speaking the truth in love, we will grow to become in every respect the mature body of him who is the head, that is, Christ. From him the whole body, joined and held together by every supporting ligament, grows and builds itself up in love, as each part does its work.

Here, the word *head* illustrates that Christ is the *source* of the church's unity and growth. It is Jesus in whom we live and move and have our being. So, Paul's emphasis is specifically on spiritual and relational flourishing. If, because of Christ, the church is being built up and able to grow, then this is how husbands should love their wives—in a way that causes her to grow and flourish!

Everything in this chapter (and the entire book of Ephesians) up to this point has been about unity and oneness: one new humanity, one body of Christ, one church—all made possible through Christ's submission to the Father, and our following his example through mutual submission. It is important to keep this front and center as we read these verses about mutual submission.

Paul's intent is that of unity, not of domination, as he parallels these relationships:

❖ Christ—Church
❖ Head—Body
❖ Husband—Wife

Christ is indeed the head—the Savior—the source of all goodness—of the church. And the head is the source of flourishing for the body. Without a head, our bodies wouldn't exactly be thriving! In this way, the husband is the head of the wife. He should always keep the unity of their marriage at the forefront of his mind, actions, and decisions—his life should be the source of her flourishing as he loves, serves, and prays daily for his wife.

N. T. Wright writes about this kind of unity when he says,

> Male and Female represent a differentiated unity—a signpost to all . . . and when they finally come together, that will be cause for rejoicing in the same way that a wedding is: a creational sign that God's project is going forwards; that opposite poles within creation are made for union, not competition. [3]

The goal of this passage is not to create rigid gender roles within marriage. And it most definitely is not about teaching women to be subjugated to men or dominated by them. This passage is about the mystery of unity within marriage and within the church—one that should reflect Christ's love. Ephesians 5 is echoing the message Paul emphasizes in every single letter he writes—that our utmost goal must always be for the unity of the church and the spread of the gospel.

When a husband and wife come together in a faithful, loving marriage that embodies mutual submission, this is a clear testimony of who God is and what God can do through Christ and the church. This type of mutual submission, modeled after the relationship of Christ and his church, is a beautiful picture of the gospel, challenging cultural norms in every society on earth.

CONCLUSION

Paul concludes this example of the marriage union as a means of mutual submission by looking at unity in an even deeper way. In verse 31 he states, "For this reason a man will leave his father and mother and be united to his wife, and the two will become one flesh." This "two becoming one" is a significant part of the covenant. They are no longer separate beings—they are now considered the same substance.

As C. S. Lewis writes in *Mere Christianity:*

> The Christian idea of marriage is based on Christ's words that a man and wife are to be regarded as a single organism. The male and the female were made to be combined together in pairs, not simply on the sexual level, but totally combined. [4]

In all of Ephesians, including this chapter, this is Paul's primary concern. In marriage—and in the church—we are called to mutually submit to one another out of gratitude for what Jesus has done and accomplished. Our gratitude should be constant for the great mystery of the gospel: that the Father has chosen to reveal his nature and plans through sinners like you and me.

PASTORAL ENCOURAGEMENT

Many people find themselves in difficult relationships. Even if your marriage is a perfect match on paper—I can promise you it will still be filled with many challenges! For Christians, marriage is a wonderful picture of Christ's love for the church. It is important for us to remember that Christ's love for the church is not modeled on human marriage. Rather, human marriage—especially within a Christian context—is to derive its example primarily from Jesus' love for his bride.

One implication is that we shouldn't perpetuate the sins of our parents. Just because your dad screamed and yelled doesn't make that permissible for you. Just because your mom was emotionally withdrawn doesn't make it permissible for you to withhold yourself from your spouse. Nor does your spouse's behavior give you license to treat them with mutual antagonism. To be a Christian is a difficult call, because it is the call to love as Christ has loved.

To those who are single, the discomfort of reading this passage may be in the longing to be married. Perhaps you've desired to have a husband or wife, but the Lord has not opened that door for you. That too can be an extremely difficult road to walk. Please know your call is no less holy, important, or sanctified from that of your married brothers and sisters. If you are in Christ, then you are wed to him. That doesn't always take away the sting of longing, but it is a sacred and holy call.

Much more can be said about mutual submission. Stay tuned for the discussion in the following chapter!

DISCUSSION QUESTIONS

1. Have you ever given this passage much thought before reading it here? Did you come at it with any preconceived ideas? Is there anything that has been either resolved or more "stirred up" after reading this chapter?

2. Has there ever been a time when you have submitted to someone "out of reverence for Christ"? What was the result of that?

3. If you are married, perhaps consider asking your spouse how you can love them better. Be ready to listen and receive what they have to say.

4. What are some healthy examples of mutual submission from your life or experience? Have you had a parent, teacher, or friend model this type of love in a beautiful way?

5. What are some contemporary "house codes" that are common in our American culture? In what ways do you think Paul might challenge these practices with a fuller picture of the gospel at work in relationships?

SPIRITUAL PRACTICES TO CONSIDER
FOR EPHESIANS 5:21–33

❖ **Intercession.** Simply put, intercession is praying for others—bringing their cares and needs to the feet of Jesus, like the men who lowered their paralyzed friend through the roof. Spend some time praying for your marriage (if married). Then pray for the marriages of the couples in your life. Ask the Holy Spirit to guide your prayers and give you insights as you join with him in his redemptive work and trust him to accomplish it in your life and in their lives.

❖ **Make a list.** Make a list of all the ways Christ has loved you and sacrificed for you. Just the act of writing these many blessings down will encourage and strengthen your soul.

12

Mutual Submission: The Gospel in Action

Ryan Stockton

EPHESIANS 6:1–9

¹ Children, obey your parents in the Lord, for this is right.
² "Honor your father and mother"—which is the first commandment with a promise— ³ "so that it may go well with you and that you may enjoy long life on the earth."

⁴ Fathers, do not exasperate your children; instead, bring them up in the training and instruction of the Lord.

⁵ Slaves, obey your earthly masters with respect and fear, and with sincerity of heart, just as you would obey Christ. ⁶ Obey them not only to win their favor when their eye is on you, but as slaves of Christ, doing the will of God from your heart. ⁷ Serve wholeheartedly, as if you were serving the Lord, not people, ⁸ because you know that the Lord will reward each one for whatever good they do, whether they are slave or free.

⁹ And masters, treat your slaves in the same way. Do not threaten them, since you know that he who is both their Master and yours is in heaven, and there is no favoritism with him.

STARTING IN THE MIDDLE

AVE YOU EVER STARTED A movie right in the middle? Maybe a friend was watching a film, and having nothing better to do, you plopped down on the couch next to them and jumped in on the story right at the halfway point. At first, things are completely chaotic. You don't know the characters, you don't know the plot, you don't understand why people are acting the ways they are, and you don't know the relational dynamics. Eventually you find your bearings and even enjoy the remainder of the movie. But missing out on the first half of the story makes it so much harder to understand the whole.

This is our situation as we begin Ephesians chapter 6. If we read chapter 6 removed from its larger context, we are jumping into a conversation that has vital information missing. We cannot read this chapter in isolation. We must remember that the chapter and verse numbers found in our modern Bibles were not a part of the original texts of Scripture. And while chapters and verses are helpful tools, sometimes the divides they make are artificial and create more confusion than clarity. Such is the case for the division between chapters 5 and 6.

We enter chapter 6 in the middle of the thought flowing from chapters 4 and 5. In those chapters, Paul unpacks what life in Christ looks like pertaining to specific relationships. We are told to speak truthfully (Eph. 4:25), not to steal from others (Eph. 4:28), to communicate in ways that build others up (Eph. 4:29), to be sexually pure (Eph. 5:3), and to not be greedy (Eph. 5:3).

In Ephesians 5:21 Paul gets to the most common of all relationships—the family. And as we saw previously, the over-arching principle when it comes to these relationships is mutual submission. If we're going to have the same mindset as Jesus, mutual submission is key. Paul writes in a different letter,

> Therefore if you have any encouragement from being united with Christ, if any comfort from his love, if any common sharing in the Spirit, if any tenderness and compassion, then make my joy complete by being like-minded, having the same love, being one in spirit and of one mind. Do nothing out of selfish ambition or vain conceit. Rather, in humility value others above yourselves, not looking to your own interests but each of you to the interests of the others.
>
> In your relationships with one another, have the same mindset as Christ Jesus: Who, being in very nature God, did not consider equality with God something to be used to his own advantage; rather, he made himself nothing by taking the very nature of a servant, being made in human likeness. And being found in appearance as a man, he humbled himself by becoming obedient to death—even death on a cross! (Phil. 2:1–8)

RELATIONSHIPS IN CHAPTER 6

This principle of mutual submission not only covers the instructions for the relationships in Ephesians 5 (wives and husbands), but also the relationships that begin chapter 6—children, fathers (parents), slaves (employees), and masters (employers).

CHILDREN:

First, children are told to obey their parents "in the Lord." What in the world does this mean? Well, unfortunately for any kids reading this, it doesn't mean you must only obey your parents if they are godly and doing everything right. This section has less to do with the worthiness of the parents and more to do with the character of the child. A child who has a relationship with Christ should emulate the mindset of Jesus and put others ahead of themselves and obey their parents.

Now, this must be said: if the parent is asking dangerous things of the child or putting them in positions that would harm them physically, emotionally, or mentally, that must not continue. But that is not what Paul is talking about here. This is describing a family as it behaves in "normal" circumstances.

In our modern context, obedience and honor often clash with the dominant cultural value of independence. Teenagers are told to "find themselves," sometimes in ways that disregard parental guidance altogether. Yet Paul's words remind us that honoring parents does not have to stifle individuality but can in fact provide a foundation for healthy independence. A child who learns respect at home often grows into an adult who treats co-workers, spouses, and friends with the same dignity. Conversely, parents must realize their role is not simply to demand obedience but to cultivate an environment where children flourish. Encouragement, patience, and consistent love do far more to shape character than a thousand sharp words ever will. Speaking of parents . . .

FATHERS:

Next, we see a command given to fathers not to exasperate their children. As a father to three children myself, I might add this: Uh oh.

I have exasperated my children before. I don't know what happened! I think the sun got in my eyes or something.

No, I know exactly what happened: sin. I fell to it again. I yielded to my selfishness and pride, placing myself ahead of my children. Whether it was my desire for a quiet moment, immediate obedience, or respect, I was not putting their needs above my own.

And just as the instruction for the children to obey their parents is not contingent on the parent's worthiness, so too my duty to put my children's needs above my own is not contingent upon whether I think they deserve it or not. I must respond with Christ-like character and love and not exasperate my children.

The warning against exasperating our kids doesn't mean we can't offer correction or guidance. But there's a difference between correction that crushes and discipline that builds up. When a father constantly points out what his child does wrong without affirming what they do right, resentments build and fester. But when correction comes with encouragement, like praising effort even when the outcome isn't perfect, children grow resilient and secure. The Christian father, then, images God the Father, who does not provoke us to despair but disciplines us in love so we can share in his holiness (Heb. 12:9–10).

SLAVES AND MASTERS:

While those two previous relationships are challenging enough, we next come to a set of relationships that are even trickier: slaves and masters. While slavery was a common enough occurrence in Paul's day as to be added to the familial relationships and house codes listed here, those of us reading from a modern perspective might wish this discussion wasn't included. But it is here, so let's take a look.

First, slaves are told to obey their masters with respect and fear. This isn't so much about trembling and fear for your life; this was actually a phrase that simply meant respect or deference due to one's higher position of authority. Slaves are also told to obey with sincerity of heart and to serve wholeheartedly.

Now, I could talk here about how slavery in the ancient Roman world was not like the chattel slavery of the American South. I could talk about how different an institution it was in ancient Rome and how people could make a living as slaves, you could get married, or how you could even work your way out of slavery. But the fact remains, slavery is slavery and we as followers of Jesus are people of freedom. So, we must oppose the institution of slavery wherever and however it exists, full stop.

With that said, some of us might wonder why Paul doesn't just undercut the whole thing right here instead of talking about how to be a "good slave" or "good master." I would prefer he did that too. But notice the instructions he gives to the masters: "And masters, treat your slaves *in the same way*" (emphasis added).

In the same way! So basically, we take what was said to the slaves and apply that to the masters. This means the masters are to treat their slaves with respect and fear, with sincerity of heart, acting as a slave of Christ, and to serve them wholeheartedly. And Paul goes even further and adds that masters are not to threaten their slaves.

So yes, I would have preferred Paul just undercut the whole institution of slavery right here. But in this instruction, he essentially levels the playing field between slave and master. And even if the distinction of "slave" and "master" was still being made culturally, in their kingdom relationship, there was mutual submission and respect as in any other relationship.

Incidentally, we see more of Paul's view of slavery in his letter to Philemon. In this letter, Paul writes to a slave owner about receiving his former slave back as an equal, even a "dear brother." Life in the kingdom models to the world a new way to live and interact with other image-bearers.

WHAT ABOUT TODAY?

Unfortunately, the desire to dominate others seems to be a growing cultural virtue. This can look like proving one's strength, being tough, not showing emotion, or eschewing compassion for harsh indifference and cruelty. These approaches to life create an atmosphere of selfishness and mistrust.

Paul's teaching at the beginning of Ephesians 6 is good medicine for our sick world. And it would have been the same back in ancient Rome. To see husbands and wives acting all "Ephesians 5-y" would have been wildly counter-cultural. To see slaves and masters acting all "Ephesians 6-y" would have been a shock to the system. Can you envision family units acting in this way?

Can you imagine any relationship acting in these ways? It would be like a breath of fresh air, a cool breeze on the face of someone too-long shut inside. It would impart life to those in these relationships.

And what about other relationships, like at work or school? The workplace becomes a natural arena where Paul's vision takes shape. Employees can choose to serve not just for a paycheck but as though serving Christ himself.

Christian employers are called to view their workers not as cogs in a machine but as image-bearers entrusted to their care. Imagine a company where promotions are motivated by recognizing potential rather than exploiting output, or where a manager sacrifices a personal bonus so their team can thrive. Perhaps they take time out of their schedule to show their employees they matter by taking them to lunch or even just stopping by their offices for a chat. As a former minion in a sea of cubicles who had bosses that treated their employees with respect and care, I can tell you this does wonders for morale and the building of relationships and trust.

The same goes for relationships at school. Students can obey teachers out of reverence for Christ. Teachers can honor their students and treat them with respect and kindness and understanding. And fellow students can respect each other, learn from each other, and hold each other up instead of forming factions, gossiping, or hurting each other.

Such practices can breathe kingdom values even into corporate and school culture.

PUTTING FEET ON OUR DOCTRINE

At the end of the day, mutual submission is what our faith looks like in action. We can talk about our beliefs and ponder doctrines all day long, but if we aren't loving other image-bearers well, if we aren't living out the love of Jesus in our relationships, what are we even doing?

Think about it. How often do conflicts erupt simply because no one wants to yield? Two friends both want their way, and the relationship strains under stubbornness. Yet when we choose humility, space opens for reconciliation. Churches too are healthiest when leaders listen more than they command, and when members seek to serve rather than be served. This is not weakness; it is the strength of Christ, who chose the way of the cross over coercive power. Can I say this again? Mutual submission is not weakness. To live as Christ calls us to live toward one another is the strongest possible posture for the human soul.

In our families, can we picture a dinner table where parents and children alike speak words that build up, where disagreements are handled with grace rather than shouting matches? Can we imagine workplaces where bosses advocate for employees' well-being above profit margins? Can we envision churches marked not by competition for influence but by joyful cooperation? These pictures may sound idealistic, but Paul wrote them not as fairy tales but as Spirit-empowered possibilities for communities shaped by Christ.

Mutual submission subverts unhealthy hierarchies, promotes meaningful communication and reasonable debate, lifts others up, and engages us in loving respect for each other. Mutual submission exercises godly dominion over worldly domination through the upside-down power of the kingdom of God.

OUR JESUS EXAMPLE

Jesus held ultimate authority. How did he wield it? Check out John 13:3–5: "Jesus knew that the Father had put all things under his power, and that he had come from God and was returning to God; so, he got up from the meal, took off his outer clothing, and wrapped a towel around his waist. After that, he poured water into a basin and began to wash his disciples' feet."

Did you catch that? Jesus knew the Father had put everything under his power, and what does he do with that knowledge? He wraps a towel around his waist and washes his friends' feet.

What? Jesus, that's not what you do with power! You're supposed to dominate your enemies and make everyone else do what you want them to! You're supposed to force people to pray to you even if they don't want to! You're supposed to find ways to reach the highest levels of human influence to do some good in this world!

Nope. The kingdom of God plays by different rules because Jesus is an utterly different type of ruler. In the kingdom, it isn't money that rules hearts and sets agendas, it is love and service. In the kingdom, it isn't politicians who wield the most power, but rather those who look and act the most like the King. Power in the kingdom means becoming a servant and, everybody say it with me, *mutual submission.*

PASTORAL ENCOURAGEMENT

Look for opportunities to serve those in your sphere of influence. Jesus said, "The Son of Man did not come to be served, but to serve, and to give his life as a ransom for many" (Matt. 20:28). Christ is the ultimate picture of mutual submission. Paul, picking up on this same theme elsewhere, writes,

> In your relationships with one another, have the same mindset as Christ Jesus: Who, being in very nature God, did not consider equality with God something to be used to his own advantage; rather, he made himself nothing by taking the very nature of a servant. (Phil. 2:5–7)

Can you follow that instruction this week? *In your relationships with one another, have the same mindset as Christ Jesus.*

DISCUSSION QUESTIONS

1. How have you personally experienced the difference between correction that builds up and correction that tears down?

2. Ephesians 6 instructs both slaves and masters to serve with sincerity of heart, "as if serving the Lord." How might this principle translate to modern workplace relationships?

3. What challenges arise when trying to live out mutual submission in settings where hierarchy and authority are expected (such as work or family life)?

4. Paul does not abolish slavery directly but calls masters to treat slaves in the same way they expect to be treated. What does this teach us about how the gospel reshapes even entrenched cultural systems?

5. In today's world, where could you resist the cultural values of domination, cruelty, or indifference and instead model Christlike humility and service?

6. How do these teachings challenge the way you view authority figures in your life? How do they challenge the way you exercise authority over others?

7. Jesus washed his disciples' feet when "all power was given to him." What does this reveal about the true nature of power in God's kingdom?

8. As you examine your engagement at your church, how can you model mutual submission better, and/or where have you seen it modeled well?

9. Looking at your own relationships, where is God calling you to lay aside pride and practice mutual submission this week?

SPIRITUAL PRACTICES TO CONSIDER
FOR EPHESIANS 6:1–9

* **Service:** Few things bring us closer to the heart of Jesus, or to our fellow humans, as serving others. Who can you serve today? Maybe it is your spouse, child, sibling, or coworker. Look for small ways to bless others. You can also look for big ways to serve. Consider joining a local community service project. As you serve, you'll watch your heart grow in compassion toward others.
* **Giving:** Jesus said, "Where your treasure is, there your heart will be also" (Matt. 6:21). Can you say "no" to an extra trip to Starbucks this week so you can say "yes" to giving toward a person or organization in need?

13

𝔚𝔢𝔞𝔭𝔬𝔫𝔰 𝔬𝔣 𝔕𝔢𝔡𝔢𝔪𝔭𝔱𝔦𝔬𝔫

Ryan Stockton

EPHESIANS 6:10–20

[10] Finally, be strong in the Lord and in his mighty power. [11] Put on the full armor of God, so that you can take your stand against the devil's schemes. [12] For our struggle is not against flesh and blood, but against the rulers, against the authorities, against the powers of this dark world and against the spiritual forces of evil in the heavenly realms. [13] Therefore put on the full armor of God, so that when the day of evil comes, you may be able to stand your ground, and after you have done everything, to stand. [14] Stand firm then, with the belt of truth buckled around your waist, with the breastplate of righteousness in place, [15] and with your feet fitted with the readiness that comes from the gospel of peace. [16] In addition to all this, take up the shield of faith, with which you can extinguish all the flaming arrows of the evil one. [17] Take the helmet of salvation and the sword of the Spirit, which is the word of God.

[18] And pray in the Spirit on all occasions with all kinds of prayers and requests. With this in mind, be alert and always keep on praying for all the Lord's people. [19] Pray also for me, that whenever I speak, words may be given me so that I will fearlessly make known the mystery of the gospel, [20] for which I am an ambassador in chains. Pray that I may declare it fearlessly, as I should.

FLIPPING EXPECTATIONS

WE MIGHT BE TEMPTED TO think Paul is abruptly changing subjects. He moves quickly from relationships to warfare imagery. But Paul is simply describing the spiritual reality that in our fallen world there is a spiritual battle!

Often, we fail to realize we're in a battle until the arrows start flying. Most of us don't wake up in the morning thinking, *"Ah yes, another day to suit up for combat!"* Instead, we roll out of bed, pour the coffee, scroll the news, and then wonder why by 9 a.m. we already feel discouraged, distracted, or on edge. Paul reminds us here that the battle is constant, even if we don't see immediate evidence in our physical lives. The temptation to snap at a coworker, the subtle envy when a neighbor posts vacation pictures, the small compromise we justify in our finances, these are not random or coincidence. They are moments where the unseen spiritual war presses into our very normal lives.

Paul draws the minds of the early Christians in Ephesus to the picture of a Roman soldier. Living under Roman occupation, everyone would have been very familiar with the Roman soldier and the tools of their trade: armor and weapons.

Paul flips our expectations. Rather than training the young Christians in the weapons of the world, he subverts earthly uses of coercive power by explaining our battle is not actually against flesh and blood. It is a battle in the unseen realm. Our battle is not physical, it's spiritual.

Christians understand from the creation story that we are created to be physical creatures; we were uniquely designed for a physical world with embodied relationships. Though we experience the results of sin and the fall in our bodies, our bodies aren't in and of themselves wicked. Our primary enemy is never another human. Our foe is a spiritual opponent. Therefore, our weapons and tactics should be spiritual as well.

Just look at the weapons named by Paul: truth, righteousness, readiness that comes from the gospel of peace, faith, salvation, the Spirit, the Word of God, and prayer. These are all spiritual practices. Notice it doesn't say the "shield of iron" or the "sword of steel." Paul is identifying spiritual weapons. Our fight will look different than the battle tactics of the world.

Our culture often teaches us to fight with biting sarcasm, with a bigger platform, with sharper rhetoric, with sheer force of personality, or sometimes even with physical violence. Think of how common it is to weaponize social media or wield money and influence to get our own way. Yet Paul calls us to an arsenal that looks, frankly, unimpressive: prayer, truth, faith, and peace. On the surface, none of these weapons appear all that powerful. They won't help me win an online argument. But that's kind of the point: the weapons of God aren't intended to merely silence enemies, they are intended to transform them. A cutting tweet can humiliate someone in the moment, but prayer for that same person can change both hearts for eternity.

So, Paul goes through the parts of the armor and gives them a coinciding Christ-like virtue for us to "wear." It doesn't help us to try to speculate about the connection between a virtue and the specific part of the armor. Paul uses a similar analogy in 1 Thessalonians 5:8, and the breastplate and helmet are associated with different qualities. The main thing is not which part of the armor they coincide with, but simply that we understand these virtues are important.

The idea is that we will be dressed in certain qualities, and we will be trained in them. A sword in the hands of someone who has no idea how to use it is not nearly as effective as someone who knows how to wield it. A bow and arrow in my hands is just about worthless because I've not been trained with them. The soldier is taught how to use the shield and sword and bow and arrow with precision and effectiveness. As we learn the tools of our spiritual warfare, we too are encouraged to train and be ready for our moments of spiritual attack.

Daily Scripture reading, prayer, acts of service, and confession can feel routine or small, but these spiritual practices build the reflexes we need when temptation or trial strikes. The time to learn how to swing a sword is not when the enemy is already at the gate, it's now. Our small, everyday disciplines are what prepare us to fight with endurance when the day of evil comes.

LIVING UNDERWATER

But from the perspective of the world these weapons will seem foolish and ineffective. They will make little sense without the unique perspective of the Christ-follower. Truth, prayer, peace—this sounds flimsy compared to force, status, or influence. That's because the fallen world can only imagine life on its own terms. Its paradigm is worldly power.

Think of it this way: our lives are shaped by the environment we're immersed in. If the "world's way" is like living underwater, then everything about us is conditioned by that environment. Underwater, plants look different, animals move differently, even our own movements are slower and weaker. Speech doesn't travel well. Power feels diminished. This is not the environment we were made for! Yet when we're submerged, we can't imagine anything else. It feels normal, even if it's limiting.

But what happens if we step out onto dry land? Suddenly, lungs fill properly, speech is clear, and strength returns. Movements are more natural, more effective, and freer. This is what it means to live "in Christ" (2 Cor. 5:16–17, Col. 3:1–3). To be immersed in him is to breathe the air we were made for. When Jesus defines our reality, through Scripture, prayer, worship, and his Spirit, life functions the way it was meant to, and the armor of God, these spiritual tools, make more sense.

The contrast is stark. Immerse yourself in news cycles, social media outrage, or echo chambers of agreement, and you'll keep feeling like you're underwater, shaped by the currents of the world. Immerse yourself in Jesus, and your whole reality shifts. Your reflexes, values, and weapons change. What once looked odd—patience instead of retaliation, forgiveness instead of bitterness, prayer instead of rage—suddenly makes sense because you're breathing kingdom air.

History is full of people who chose "dry land" while others stayed submerged. In the book of Acts, Stephen prayed for his killers instead of cursing them. Countless believers have answered slander with grace and hatred with love. Jesus himself forgave his executioners. To those still underwater, these choices look strange, even foolish. But to those in Christ and breathing his air, they reveal the only reality that truly lasts.

OUR TOOLS AND WEAPONS

When we are in Christ, the tools and weapons of worldly warfare will feel strange and out of place in our hands. We'll even hate the effects of them when they are used. The armor of God will feel so much more natural. Remember King David when he went to fight Goliath? He was given the physical armor of a military soldier, but it just didn't fit. Instead, he went in the power of God, not the power of steel. And the victory was a double victory, one for Israel and one for the kingdom of God.

The weapons we use will determine the outcomes we achieve. When we use the weapons and tools of the world, we should not be surprised when we receive worldly outcomes. If we say with our mouths we want peace, but we try to use the means of war to get it, we shouldn't be surprised when the result is not peace, but rather additional conflict. If we say we want a restored relationship with a person, but we keep employing the tools of unforgiveness or pride, we shouldn't be surprised when the relationship remains in ruins.

If we want peace and reconciliation, we must use the tools designed by God to bring about peace and reconciliation. A house is never built using a wrecking ball; it is only torn down with one. We must choose the right tools if we're to be builders rather than participating in the continual tearing down of people, systems, and cultures.

Imagine what it would look like if we really swapped earthly weapons for Jesus' tools in our daily lives. What if, instead of wielding resentment in our marriages, we reached for prayer? What if, instead of sarcasm with our kids, we grabbed patience? What if, as churches, we were tempted less by political power and pressed more into forgiveness and hospitality? Healthy communities of faith are never built with cynicism, fear, or hostility. Only when we reach for the right tools can we construct something that lasts.

When we employ physical weapons, we will inevitably hurt fellow image-bearers. It's the nature of weapons to cause harm. We cannot help a person if we are hurting them at the same time. We cannot love a person if we are fighting them. On the flip side, we cannot harm a person if we are truly praying God's blessings and care for them. We cannot kill a person by showing them the love of Jesus through our actions. This is why Jesus, in coming to bring peace between us and heaven, employed the tools of peace, not of war.

OUR TEMPTATION TODAY

The tone of our culture's rhetoric is growing more and more extreme. Everything is a crisis, an existential threat. What we see online, what we read and hear from the highest offices of our country is so often hate, vitriol, fear, and an escalation of the stakes. We are constantly told this person is evil, or that person is taking Christianity from our country (as if God was dependent on a country or national strength).

When the stakes are raised so high, we are tempted to fight physically. We are tempted to use the same weapons as those arrayed against us. But where do we see fear, or actual physical swords listed as part of the armor of God? This passage reminds us quite starkly that the world of fear and violence is not to be the reality of followers of Jesus. Of course we are affected by these things, but these are not the tools of choice for a Christ follower.

Our digital age makes this even harder. The "weapons of the world" are just a thumb-swipe away. We rage-post, doom-scroll, and argue in comment sections as if we were defending the honor of God himself. But none of these activities are listed in Paul's armor. There's no "breastplate of the perfect clapback" or "sword of the meme." In fact, using these weapons often just entangles us deeper in the world's miry bog. What would it look like if, instead of feeding the outrage machine, we prayed for those who stir it? What if our online presence was marked less by fear and fury and more by peace and patience? That would be truly countercultural, and deeply Christlike.

Remember the list here: truth, righteousness, readiness that comes from the gospel of peace, faith, salvation, the Spirit, the Word of God, prayer. And this is not an exhaustive list. This partners with other virtues we see in the New Testament:

things like humility, integrity, and the fruit of the Spirit (love, joy, peace, patience, kindness, goodness, faithfulness, gentleness, self-control). These are our means of living in this world.

KEEP FIGHTING

Sometimes, choosing the right thing might feel like losing. We might live out these virtues and feel like those who are employing the weapons of the world are getting stronger or "winning." And for a while, that might indeed be the case. But ultimately, we stand before God. We will live eternally in the kingdom and only temporarily in our country.

God sees it all. His justice reigns and will come. It may not arrive on our timeline, but it comes, and it arrives with perfect timing. No one "gets away" with anything. All will stand before the judgment seat of Christ. Stay faithful. This is the message of the book of Revelation as well. We see the countless followers of Jesus being urged to stay faithful. God will fight the battles, and he will bring the victories. Stay faithful and fight the fight of the Spirit.

All of this could feel overwhelming if we thought it depended solely on us. But two encouragements urge us to keep going. The first is that Paul's imagery shows us this is not our armor. It is God's armor, gifted to us. We don't strap on righteousness by sheer willpower or conjure up faith by trying harder. We receive these pieces from the One who already won the ultimate battle through the cross and resurrection.

The second encouragement is that not only are we fighting under the power of God, but we are fighting alongside those who claim Christ as their Lord. There will be days when I am too depleted to lift the sword of the Spirit. But others who are stronger can come alongside me. And on other days, I will bear the shield of faith well for others when they struggle. In the body of Christ, we fight the spiritual battles together.

The invitation is not to be superhuman, but to stay connected to God who is our source of strength, and to his people who fight these battles with us. When you feel too weak to fight, that's okay; God gives us himself and his people. I am thankful that this faithful God never leaves us or forsakes us as we work to bring his kingdom here like it is in heaven.

PASTORAL ENCOURAGEMENT

The language in Ephesians 6 is plural. So, when Paul says, "put on the armor of God," he is saying "all of you, together, put on the armor." It is not possible to "stand firm" in isolation. Together we put on the breastplate of righteousness. Together we put on the helmet of salvation. Together we put on the boots of the good news. Together we hold the shield of faith. Together we wield the sword of the Spirit. Together we buckle on the belt of truth. Lean into Christian relationships and community. Ask for help. Put yourself in healthy accountability structures. Encourage one another. Together, stand firm.

DISCUSSION QUESTIONS

1. Paul reminds us our struggle is not against "flesh and blood" but against spiritual forces. How does this shift your perspective on the challenges you face in daily life?

2. Which piece of the armor of God (truth, righteousness, peace, faith, salvation, the Spirit, the Word, prayer) feels most natural for you to "wear," and which feels hardest? Why?

3. How do you typically recognize when you are in the midst of a spiritual battle? Do you tend to see it only after the "arrows start flying"?

4. What are some "worldly weapons" (sarcasm, power, rhetoric, social media attacks, etc.) you've been tempted to use instead of God's weapons?

5. Spiritual training can be compared to an athlete practicing or a musician rehearsing. What daily spiritual "drills" help build your reflexes for battle?

6. Paul's imagery reminds us the armor is God's, not ours. How does that truth encourage you when you feel weak or inadequate?

7. What does it look like in your life to be "immersed in Christ" instead of "immersed in the world"?

8. When do you find yourself most tempted to "fight like the world" (online interactions, workplace stress, family conflict, politics)?

9. When living out Christlike virtues feels like "losing," how do you hold onto hope that God's justice and victory will ultimately prevail?

10. Looking ahead at your next week, where do you see opportunities to practice with one of these spiritual weapons more intentionally?

SPIRITUAL PRACTICES TO CONSIDER FOR EPHESIANS 6:10–20

❖ **Meditate:** In your imagination, slowly put on each piece of armor listed by Paul in Ephesians 6. As you get dressed in the armor, notice in which areas you need the most help. Perhaps you feel confident of the truth of Christ, but your breastplate of righteousness seems flimsy. As you notice your areas of need, pray to the Lord for further growth and maturity.

❖ **Encourage:** Encourage someone else today. Write a note, send a text, or pick up the phone. Someone in your life needs encouragement. Encouragement from a brother or sister in Christ is a powerful way to help one another put on the full armor of God. Help a brother out! Aid a sister! And thank God when someone else does the same for you.

14

Undying Love

D. Jay Martín

EPHESIANS 6:21–24

²¹ Tychicus, the dear brother and faithful servant in the Lord, will tell you everything, so that you also may know how I am and what I am doing. ²² I am sending him to you for this very purpose, that you may know how we are, and that he may encourage you.

²³ Peace to the brothers and sisters, and love with faith from God the Father and the Lord Jesus Christ. ²⁴ Grace to all who love our Lord Jesus Christ with an undying love.

FAREWELL!

IN MY EARLIER CHAPTER ON Ephesians 1, way back at the beginning of this book, I told the story of the identity crisis I experienced as a young man. In moving across the world, multiple times, I had to rediscover my identity within the context of a new place and culture. One thing I learned during these cross-world transitions is the gut-wrenching difficulty of saying a long-term "goodbye."

It's one thing to say, "See ya later!" to a friend we'll run into next weekend at our kid's baseball game. It's another thing to say, "I love you and I'll miss you so much," to a grandparent that you know you won't see for several years. When I first moved to the Philippines in 1997, my great-grandma, Opal Fleetwood, was still alive. I prayed she would live long enough for me to see her again. She did! In fact, I got to spend quite a bit more time with her. She continued to live independently and kept a large garden at her home in rural Missouri until she passed at the age of ninety-eight.

Paul's final words in Ephesians are closer to that second type of farewell. These early Christians lived in a world without cell phones, FaceTime calls, or emails. There was no airplane travel or major highways to ease long distance visits. Paul was in prison, and unsure of what would come next in his life. And so, he closes with heartfelt words of love and blessing.

Colossians 4:7–8 and Ephesians 6:21–22 are nearly identical. In both texts Tychicus is personally named as Paul's commissioned letter carrier. Many scholars believe Ephesians, Colossians, and Philemon were written around the same time. So, it could be that Tychicus traveled carrying all three letters, in one big journey. A type of official mail system existed in the Roman Empire; however, private letters—which Ephesians would have qualified as—needed to be sent by private means. Tychicus was the man for the job. [1]

In several of Paul's other letters he closes with greetings to a list of specific people. Romans and Colossians are both examples of this, as these two letters conclude with personal greetings to various people and households. Ephesians doesn't end with a list of people's names. Instead, it wraps up with a few simple but meaningful lines about the peace, love, and grace of Jesus.

To receive a letter written by a beloved brother, originating from another city in the Roman Empire, would have been a major event for these early Christians! Paul had close relationships with many of the believers in Ephesus and his love for them is evident throughout the letter. The depth of his affection is palpable in the closing words of Ephesians. Meditate for a moment on the emotional power of the final two sentences of the letter. "Peace to the brothers and sisters, and love with faith from God the Father and the Lord Jesus Christ. Grace to all who love our Lord Jesus Christ with an undying love."

For the remainder of this chapter, we'll look more closely at these two sentences and unpack how they still apply to us today.

PEACE TO THE BROTHERS AND SISTERS

Peace is a loaded word in English. When reading the word *peace*, you may immediately think of the termination of violence, the ending of a specific conflict, a treaty between two previously warring nations, or two fingers lifted high in the air by a hippy with long hair and far-out sunglasses.

Peace was a loaded word for Paul too. The letter was written in Greek, and the word here is *eirene*. Like the English word *peace*, the primary, non-Christian use of the word had to do with tranquility or harmony between various factions. But Paul of course was a Jew. And so, humming in the background for Paul was the Hebrew word *shalom*.

Shalom can also describe an ending of violence, but it means much more than that too. It has to do with the idea of spiritual and relational wholeness, of things operating and existing as they were meant to. Christians believe that when Christ returns and remakes both the heavens and the earth, all creation will exist in a perpetual state of *shalom*—peace, harmony, wholeness. Things will be as they were meant to be, functioning fully according to God's design, without blemish.

The New Testament writers began to use the Greek word *eirene* in much the same way, importing the significance of *shalom* from the Hebrew Scriptures. When Paul writes, "peace to the brothers and sisters," it isn't just a flippant "peace out, dudes!" Instead, it is packed with all the meaning and the implications of the work of Christ described in the previous chapters of the letter.

In Ephesians 1:2, Paul began the letter with the statement, "Grace and peace to you from God our Father and the Lord Jesus Christ." In Ephesians 2:14–16, when describing the unifying work of Christ among Jews and Gentiles, Paul writes,

> For he himself is our peace, who had made the two groups one and has destroyed the barrier, the dividing wall of hostility . . . His purpose was to create in himself one new humanity out of the two, thus making peace, and in this one body to reconcile both of them to God through the cross, by which he put to death their hostility.

In Ephesians 2:17 Paul says, "He came and preached peace to you who were far away and peace to those who were near." In Ephesians 4:3 he writes, "Make every effort to keep the unity of the Spirit through the bond of peace." And in Ephesians 6:14–15, "Stand firm then . . . with your feet fitted with the readiness that comes from the gospel of peace."

Thus, when Paul writes, "Peace to the brothers and sisters," it is a phrase packed with significance.

The peace of Christ is a sign of your reconciliation both to God and to your brothers and sisters. It testifies to God's redemptive work in your life. It points to your freedom from sin. It fills you with hope and assurance for the eternal salvation you have in Jesus. And it prepares your feet to share the gospel. What a gift the peace of Christ is!

In Colossians 3:15 Paul writes, "Let the peace of Christ rule in your hearts, since as members of one body you were called to peace. And be thankful." The peace of Christ—the wholeness and rightness he accomplishes in our lives—is meant to "rule" in our hearts.

LOVE WITH FAITH

Pastor Tasha Hoover wrote beautifully about God's love in her chapters detailing Ephesians 3. In those chapters she explored four different Greek words used to describe various types of love. You may remember in Ephesians, Paul uses the word *agape* to define God's love for us.

Once again, in the closing lines of the letter, Paul draws from this same well. He can't help himself. Every time Paul opens his mouth in conversation, or begins dictating a letter, or prays, he is continually drawn back to the incredible *agape*-love of God in Christ.

Whether or not you feel like it, you are loved by God. And, in Christ, that love is unconditional. If you have a relationship with Jesus Christ as Lord and Savior, then when God the Father looks upon you, he sees the righteousness of his Son Jesus coursing through your veins. This is not because you are already perfect in your own strength, nor have you completely ceased from struggling with sin. Rather, you are unconditionally loved because God has imparted to you his own righteousness in Christ, making you worthy of his love by his own choice and volition.

In one of the most breathtakingly beautiful moments in all of Paul's writings, he says in Ephesians 2:4–6,

> But because of his great love for us, God, who is rich in mercy, made us alive with Christ even when we were dead in transgressions—it is by grace you have been saved. And God raised us up with Christ and seated us with him in the heavenly realms in Christ Jesus.

What Greek word do you think is translated into English as "love" here in Ephesians 2? Of course, it is *agape*. It is a word that appears ten times in the six chapters of Ephesians. In

Christ, you are loved, and because you are loved, you are freed from sin and fully adopted into the family of God.

Now, the phrase here in Ephesians 6:23 is specifically, "love *with* faith." That is an interesting combination. I might expect Paul to say, "love *and* faith." But he expressly writes, "Peace to the brothers and sisters, and love *with* faith from God" (emphasis added). Why?

In 1 Corinthians 13:13 Paul writes, "And now these three remain: faith, hope and love. But the greatest of these is love." I think Paul is expressing the same thing in Ephesians 6:23. Love that is truly representative and authentic to the love of Christ will always be accompanied by faith. The love of Christ cannot be separated from the gift of faith.

Faith has become one of my favorite words, but for a long time I've wrestled with it. I am the son of evangelical missionaries, I attended evangelical Bible colleges, and I am an evangelical-seminary–trained pastor. It probably will come as no surprise that the word *faith* has been an almost daily part of my vocabulary throughout the entirety of my life.

The reason the English word *faith* has bothered me at times is because of what it has come to mean in popular culture. Were you or I to walk out onto the street and ask the first person we saw, "What does it mean to have faith?" The answer would likely be something close to, "It means believing something that you have no proof for." In an age of technology and modern science, faith has been largely boiled down to superstitious beliefs for religious fanatics. Faith and science have been juxtaposed as if they are oil and water, impossible to fully mix.

Friends, can I offer a bit of relief from this oversimplistic madness? Believing in something there is no proof for is *not* what having faith in God means. The Greek word we translate as "faith" is *pistis*. It can mean "belief," "fidelity," "faithfulness," and even "allegiance."

Caesar, the ruler of the Roman Empire, demanded *pistis* from his subjects. I don't think Caesar cared one bit if his subjects believed in him without proof. Rather, he cared that they paid their taxes, performed their duties, didn't cause trouble, and obeyed his commands. In short, Caesar demanded *pistis* because he wanted loyal, faithful subjects. [2]

Here it is worth quoting N.T. Wright at length from his book *Paul: A Biography.*

> For Paul, the word [*pistis*] meant all of that but also much more. For him, this "believing allegiance" was neither simply a "religious" stance nor a "political" one. It was altogether larger, in a way that our language, like Paul's, has difficulty expressing clearly. For him, this *pistis*, this heartfelt trust in and allegiance to the God revealed in Jesus, was the vital marker, the thing that showed whether someone was really part of this new community or not. [3]

And so, when the early Christian writers invite us into a life of *faith*, they are not asking us to follow God without proof of his existence. Rather, they are saying, "God raised Jesus from the dead! We saw him with our own eyes, we spoke to him in the flesh! Everything has changed now. Death has been defeated. There is a new way to be human. He is the risen and glorified King. Jesus is the Messiah. We owe him everything—our belief, our loyalty, our faithfulness, our obedience, our allegiance."

To have faith in God is to offer him our believing loyalty in response to his mercy and grace. This understanding of faith has been transformative for me in my walk with the Lord. Of course, Jesus wants me to believe him, but he also wants me to obey him. This understanding of faith leaves room for me to wrestle with God and ask hard questions, and sometimes even struggle with doubts.

Pistis means I have a believing loyalty to King Jesus, and I want to be faithful to his teachings and commands. I think this is why Paul writes, "Peace to the brothers and sisters, and love *with* faith from God the Father and the Lord Jesus Christ."

GRACE TO ALL WHO LOVE OUR LORD JESUS CHRIST WITH AN UNDYING LOVE

Grace is a word equally loaded with meaning and import—rivaling even "peace," "love," and "faith." Grace is the means by which the love of God first comes to us. Grace is the essence of the famous verse, "But God demonstrates his own love for us in this: While we were still sinners, Christ died for us" (Romans 5:8).

We access, or step into, God's love and grace through our faith in him. Faith is the act—the believing loyalty—that allows us to fully enter into the story of God's love. Faith is an acceptance, an unwrapping of the present God gives us by his grace. To hear the gospel and to not accept the grace of God through faith is like receiving a new car for Christmas and leaving it wrapped up and sitting in the driveway until it is finally repossessed.

So, let the peace of God rule in your hearts. May the love of God, received through allegiant-faith, guide your steps. May the unearned, undeserved grace of the Lord lead you to an even deeper intimacy with Christ—an undying love.

There is a poetic beauty in the phrase *undying love*. A more literal translation of the Greek would be something like, "Grace to all who love our Lord Jesus Christ in immortality." The major English translations have various ways of handling this unusual phrase. In the NIV it is rendered "Grace to all who love our Lord Jesus Christ with an undying love."

The main idea Paul seems to be highlighting is the eternality of Jesus. And because Jesus lives eternally, and because we are raised to new life in him and share in the hope of his glory, our love for him has become an immortal, undying love. Regardless, the phrase *undying love* is beautiful and worth meditating on.

Jesus is undying. His love for us is eternal. In Christ we share this eternal, resurrection hope. Thus, our love for Christ, and his love for us, is undying. And all those who love Christ can be assured of his *peace, love,* and *grace* not only in this life, but in eternity.

WHAT I HOPE YOU WILL TAKE AWAY

As we wrap up our study in the book of Ephesians, here are a few of the things I hope you will keep with you for the rest of your life. These five highlighted points best explain why I wanted us to write this book in the first place.

KNOW YOUR IDENTITY IN CHRIST:

I hope in reading and studying Ephesians you have a better understanding, and thus a deeper appreciation, for all the blessings God has bestowed upon you in Christ. You are chosen, forgiven, rescued from sin, redeemed, filled with the Holy Spirit, adopted, brought into the family of God, included in the church, given spiritual gifts, and covered in the armor of God.

THE MINISTRY RECONCILIATION:

A major theme of all of Paul's writing is reconciliation. In his context this most often concerned the reconciliation of Jewish/Gentile relationships. And this conversation features prominently in Ephesians. God has made one new humanity in Christ. No longer should human distinctions or cultures act as the primary guide to how we relate to one another. Jesus is creating a worldwide family that includes persons from every tribe, nation, and tongue on earth. Reconciliation should continue to be at the forefront of our lives, ministries, and churches. Any number of issues seek to divide people today. But we are a people of reconciliation because God has first reconciled us to himself. Don't be afraid to swim against the cultural streams of division.

UNITY IN THE BODY:

Closely related to reconciliation is the idea of unity and oneness of the body of Christ. In Ephesians 4:3 Paul writes, "Make every effort to keep the unity of the Spirit through the bond of peace." I doubt many of us have made every effort to keep unity! But this is our call. It is not optional. To seek and work toward unity in the body of Christ is a mandate, a commandment from the very heart of Jesus. I know this is difficult. I know this is challenging. I know it costs something. I know you can't possibly heal the fractures within the body of Christ on your own. But I am also confident you can do something—small as it may seem in your own eyes. So, within your context, with the influence God has entrusted to you, make every effort to maintain the unity of the Spirit.

MUTUAL SUBMISSION:

Closely related to reconciliation and unity is the idea of mutual submission. Christ came to serve, not to be served (Matt. 20:28). If the King of Kings, God himself, became a servant, should we not also become servants? There is a great freedom that only comes from mutual submission. When we practice this essential kingdom principle, we begin to see our small, but important, part in the story of God more clearly. We begin to elevate the needs of others. We begin to imitate Christ.

DEVOTED TO PRAYER:

Paul can hardly go a chapter without bursting into prayer. His prayers are worshipful and intercessory; that is, focused on the needs of those he prays for. One of my hopes is that as you meditate on the words of Ephesians, prayer would become an increasingly regular, moment by moment, essential element of your day. May prayer become as constant and as natural as breathing.

DISCUSSION QUESTIONS

1. Have you ever spent so much time thinking about the closing of a New Testament letter? What can you learn from the closing of one of Paul's other letters? Do you have a favorite closing benediction from a different letter in the Bible?

2. Did you learn anything new about *peace, love, faith,* or *grace?* What new insight or idea did you glean about one of these key ideas?

3. If you were writing a letter to another church, what spiritual truths or encouragement would you include in the final sentences?

4. What is one of the main things you'll be taking away from our study in Ephesians?

5. What is the most challenging part of Ephesians for you? Is there something Paul wrote that makes you uncomfortable? Do you struggle to believe something he wrote about?

6. What will change in your life because of the truth revealed in Ephesians?

SPIRITUAL PRACTICES TO CONSIDER
FOR THE BOOK OF EPHESIANS

* **Scripture Memory:** Memorization is becoming a lost art in a world of smart phones, artificial intelligence, and quick Google searches. My concern is that this holds doubly true regarding the memorization of Scripture. I am not above doing a quick search using modern tools; I do it all the time. But I thank God for the verses and stories hidden in my heart. I "own" them in a deeper way. Pick out a verse or passage from Ephesians that you don't have memorized, commit it to memory.

* **Write a Letter to a Church:** Pick a church family that you are not a part of. It could be a different church represented in this book, or one just down the street from your home. Consider writing a handwritten letter or note of encouragement to that congregation. Receiving a simple letter of blessing could be just what that church family needs this week!

About the Contributors

Justin Ryan Boyer

Justin has been in vocational ministry for eighteen years. He currently serves as a pastor locally (Cornerstone Christian Fellowship) and as a connector regionally with Netzer.org. His training is interdisciplinary and includes Biblical Studies, Business, Media Design, and Spiritual Formation. He and his wife, Naomi, have been married for twenty years and have four daughters.

Ernest Daniels Jr.

Ernest Daniels Jr. serves as Lead Pastor of Christ Community Church in Philadelphia, where his passion for people and the presence of God has shaped over twenty years of ministry. A communicator, recording artist, and author, he's dedicated to helping others experience transformation through a genuine relationship with Christ.

Tim Doering

Tim Doering is a pastor to pastors and the founder of Netzer, a cross-denominational network that strengthens the church through prayer, friendship, and collaboration. After eighteen years in local church ministry, Tim launched Netzer to encourage pastors and cultivate unity in the body of Christ. Today, Netzer hosts leadership cohorts, equipping gatherings, and regional worship and prayer events, while Tim provides coaching and counsel to leaders locally and abroad. He also co-hosts The Quiet Reformation *podcast. Tim and his wife, Jen, live in the Philadelphia area and have two college-aged sons, Evan and Kolton. Learn more at www.netzer.org.*

Matt DeMontaigne

Matt has spent the last nineteen years pastoring Valley View Community Church (after thirteen wild and wonderful years with Young Life), trying to help ordinary people bump into the incarnate Jesus in ways that actually make sense. When he's not dreaming up creative ways to keep the church gospel-true, you'll probably find him in the garage covered in sawdust, building something out of wood while Lucy and Champ (dogs) and his favorite people—Megan (wife), Ella, and Catherine (daughters)— supervise. He's convinced that in a world obsessed with polish, humility and vulnerability are where Jesus does his best work.

David Hakes

Dave Hakes has over twenty-five years of ministry experience and sixteen years of pastoral ministry in the Brethren in Christ. He enjoys spending time with his wife, Christina, and their five amazing kids! Cheering for the Phillies & Eagles, drinking good coffee, walking his dog, and keeping up with kids' activities are ways he spends his free time.

Tasha Hoover

Tasha Hoover, DMin, is the Lead Pastor of Storehouse Church in Plymouth Meeting, Pennsylvania, where she's passionate about helping people experience the fullness of Christ. Married with three incredible kids, she thrives on great tea, good books, meaningful conversation, and spontaneous dance parties—in no particular order.

D. Jay Martin

D. Jay Martin (MDiv, Liberty Theological Seminary) serves as the Pastor of Vision and Leadership at Parker Ford Church. He is a husband and dad of four. Utilizing his multicultural background and theological training, he has a passion for building bridges between various cultures and groups, both inside and outside the church.

Ruth Martin

Ruth lives in Lebanon, Pennsylvania, and works part-time as the Administrator at Cornerstone Christian Fellowship, where she also practices spiritual formation ministry. In 2023, she graduated from Gordon-Conwell Theological Seminary with a master's in Theological Studies, concentrating on the Old Testament and the New Testament.

Chris M. Slawecki

Chris M. Slawecki serves as a middle school instructor, on the worship team, as a Deacon, and helps lead the men's fellowship at Valley View Community Church. His writing has been published in various online and print publications. He is a husband, father of two, and grandfather of five.

Ryan Stockton

Ryan Stockton is the Lead Pastor at Marsh Creek Community Church, a Brethren in Christ church in Exton, Pennsylvania. He holds a master's in Theological Studies and is the husband of a wonderful wife and father to three wild kids. He co-hosts the BICLife Podcast *and writes on Substack at* Living Jesusly.

Notes

CHAPTER 2 - IDENTITY CRISIS

1. Marty Folsom, *Karl Barth's Church Dogmatics for Everyone, Volume II: The Doctrine of God* (Eugene, OR: Cascade Books, 2014), 160.

CHAPTER 4 - GRACE THROUGH FAITH

1. Mark and Patti Virkler, *The 4 Keys to Hearing God's Voice* (Shippensburg, PA: Destiny Image Publishers, 2013).

CHAPTER 8 - ONE BODY

1. Ian Harber, *Walking Through Deconstruction: How to Be a Companion in a Crisis of Faith.* (Downers Grove, IL: IVP, 2025), 81.

2. J.R. Briggs, and Bob Hyatt, *Eldership and the Mission of God: Equipping Teams for Faithful Church Leadership.* (Downers Grove, IL: IVP, 2015), 47.

CHAPTER 9 - CREATED TO BE LIKE GOD

1. F. F. Bruce, *The Epistles to the Colossians, to Philemon, and to the Ephesians* (Grand Rapids, MI: Eerdmans, 2001), 355.

2. Clinton E. Arnold, "Ephesians," in *Zondervan Illustrated Bible Backgrounds Commentary,* ed. Clinton E. Arnold, vol. 3 (Grand Rapids, MI: Zondervan, 2022), 303.

3. Arnold, 303.

4. John R. W. Stott, *The Message of Ephesians* (Downers Grove, IL: InterVarsity Press, 1979), 179.

5. Eugene H. Peterson, *Practice Resurrection* (Grand Rapids, MI: William B. Eerdmans Pub. Co, 2010), 196–197.

6. I am pulling from the Examen instructions from the book *Silencio,* edited by Stephen Macchia, as well as "A Contemplative Foundation" from Order of the Common Life (https://www.orderofthecommonlife.org/course/acf).

7. Jared Patrick Boyd, *Finding Freedom in Constraint* (Downers Grove, IL: IVP Academic, 2023), 221.

8. Boyd, 223.

CHAPTER 11 - A SPIRIT-FILLED MARRIAGE

1. Klyne Snodgrass, *Ephesians: The NIV Application Commentary* (Grand Rapids, MI: Zondervan, 1996), 293–294.

2. Ibid., 294.

3. N. T. Wright, *Surprised by Hope: Rethinking Heaven, the Resurrection, and the Mission of the Church* (New York: HarperOne, 2008), 116.

4. C.S. Lewis, *Mere Christianity* (New York: The Macmillan Company, 1952), 104–105.

CHAPTER 14 - UNDYING LOVE

1. Klyne Snodgrass, *Ephesians: The NIV Application Commentary,* (Grand Rapids, MI: Zondervan, 1996), 362.

2. N.T. Wright, *Paul: A Biography* (New York: HarperOne, 2018), 90.

3. Ibid.

Acknowledgments

A COLLABORATIVE PROJECT LIKE THIS IS only possible through the selflessness and generosity of those involved. I want to express gratefulness to all the churches and contributors who participated in this book project. Thank you for taking time out of your very busy schedules to help create this resource for our communities. Thank you to my wife, Julie, and my four kids. Thank you to Parker Ford Church's leadership, staff, and congregation for continuing to believe and support our call to be an "Antioch" church. Without your support and encouragement, I would not be able to put so much time and effort into a regionally minded project like this. Thank you to Shannon Vining for helping me work through several big issues on the book, during a very busy and stressful period. Her artistic and writing gifts were invaluable. Thank you also to Debbie Capeci at Morning Joy Media for believing and supporting this unique publishing model!

—D. Jay Martín

www.ingramcontent.com/pod-product-compliance
Lightning Source LLC
LaVergne TN
LVHW052025080426
835513LV00018B/2170